Museum of Fine Arts, Lyon
Guide to the Collections

Published with the support of
Banque Française du Commerce Extérieur

Museum of Fine Arts, Lyon
Guide to the Collections

Réunion
des Musées
Nationaux

List of Authors	Dominique Brachlianoff (D.B.)
	Christian Briend (C.B.)
	Philippe Durey (P.D.)
	Valérie Lavergne - Durey (V.D.)
	Véronique Gay (V.G.)
	Geneviève Galliano (G.G.)
	Jean-Claude Goyon (J.C.G.)
	François Planet (F.P.)
Translation	John Doherty

Contents

Among the monuments and landscapes which compose the face of a city, some are famous, and strike us by their beauty, their history or simply their dimensions. Others, less well known, are more secret, and surprise the visitor who comes across them unawares: this is where the collective memory of the inhabitants often lays down the diverse strata of an identity, generation after generation. As a landmark of Lyon, the Palais Saint Pierre, strangely, is both overt and covert. With its ambitious façade, rising up as if to hold back the avalanche of red roofs rushing down the slopes of the Croix-Rousse, the Palais establishes itself with impressive authority in the very heart of the town, on the long southern side of the Place des Terreaux. But its function is well concealed. And it is certainly not on the square itself, in front of the austere proportions of its façade, that one will find the real "lieu de mémoire".

This locus of memory is more likely to be located within, somewhat hidden behind the dark vault of the porch, through which the subdued light of a garden and the white stone of a fountain — an antique sarcophagus crowned by a green bronze statue — can be made out. This is where the symbol is to be found, in the smiling serenity of a cloistered garden filled with statues, sheltered from the bustle of the town, hidden from the busy life of the streets by the solemn wall of the façade. The Museum of Fine Arts and its huge collections — "the great moral archives of the town", to use Focillon's striking words[1] — have been housed for two centuries around the cloister, in what used to be the noble Benedictine abbey of the Dames de Saint Pierre. The vaults of the cloister, where the names of Lyonnais artists now make up a sort of Pantheon, were at one time covered with "beautiful funerary or votive Latin inscriptions, blackened by time", and before they were removed many years ago the gallery must have looked "similar to the 'vias' of ancient Rome, whose monuments to the dead were an exhortation, a lesson and an example". For Focillon, "no museum vestibule is as moving as this one... Michelet would have liked it. His footsteps, echoing on the paving stones, would have called forth great shadows and great lessons."[2] The inscriptions are now more securely housed at the top of the hill of Fourvière, in the new museum of Gallo-Roman civilisation. And the walls of the cloister have been restored to their monastic austerity, relieved only by the polychromy of the vaults. Today the garden, with its pensive statues, bronze medallions, its mosaics and the casts of its arches, has become the indispensable "vestibule", a preserved space where visitors can rest their eyes and free their spirits. The unique character of the museum comes out first and foremost in this particular harmony, forged by time, between a monument and a function for which it was not designed.

The site was only given its present configuration in the seventeenth century. Of the ancient stones of the convent of "Saint Pierre les Nonnains", apparently founded in the sixth century, all that is left is a magnificent twelfth century Romanesque porch. In 1659, Anne de Chaulnes (c. 1625-1672), a determined and ambitious abbess, daughter of a Marshal of France, decided to entirely transform the building. The plans were drawn up by an architect from Avignon, François Royers de la Valfenière (1575-1667), who was already quite old and who made this his masterpiece, particularly the monumental elevation of the main façade on the Place des Terreaux, and the two lateral façades. At the death of Anne de Chaulnes, there were still two wings to be built, and the task was taken up by her sister Antoinette (1633-1708), who had succeeded her as abbess. She called on a painter and architect, Thomas Blanchet (1614-1689), who, after his return from Italy in 1655, had become the great organiser of Lyonnais decoration, and who had just demonstrated the richness and breadth of his talent on the ceilings of the Town Hall. All that remain of his work at Saint Pierre are the splendid grand stairway, which after its recent restoration is once more illuminated by its five windows, and the extraordinary baroque exuberance of the refectory, which has few equivalents in France. He employed talented stuccoists such as Simon Guillaume, Nicolas Bidault and Marc Chabry, as well as Pierre-Louis Cretey (c. 1645- after 1690), a strange painter who worked in a tormented style and whose originality is slowly being rediscovered today.

This imposing decor remained more or less unchanged until 1789; but the Revolution, during which the last nuns were forced to leave, radically changed the use of the building. The idea of turning it into a museum rapidly came to the fore, but could only be brought to fruition after the famous consular decree of 1 September 1801, which created fifteen museums outside Paris. On the banks of the Rhône, as everywhere else, the revolutionaries wanted to bring together the works of art that had been confiscated or seized from the churches, and to use them for the education of the people; however, their main concern was the manufactories, which, in Lyon, "are all based on the art of drawing". And Étienne Mayeuvre de Champvieux, deputy of the Rhône at the Conseil des Cinq Cents, had the revival of the silk industry in mind when, in 1799, he asked the government to send "some paintings from the three schools", and particularly "a few paintings by van Huysum for the study of flowers, which is an essential study for Lyon"[3] to train the designers "through the presence of artistic masterpieces". The museum was thus conceived with a utilitarian and economic aim in mind; its natural complement within the Palais Saint Pierre was a School of Drawing, which was to become the École des Beaux-Arts in 1805, and which included a "Flower Class" where students were taught how to compose patterns that would be used on silk. The State gave generously: 110 paintings were sent in 1803, 1805 and 1811 — this was the largest number sent to any provincial town. Next to masterpieces by Perugino, Veronese, Tintoretto, Guercino, Rubens, Champaigne and Jouvenet, there were sumptuous bouquets by van Brussel and de Heem, but the Lyonnais had to pay for the van Daël and van Huysum paintings that they coveted. A little before 1815, the first curator, François Artaud (1767-1838), opened a "Salon des Fleurs", close to the gallery where the works of the great masters were shown.

The objectives of the new institutions were thus clearly defined, and great efforts were made to attain them; nevertheless, an important development appeared with the restoration of the monarchy in 1814. Antiquities had been given a considerable amount of space from the beginning, but not as a result of the same economic imperatives. The archæologist François Artaud and the town councillors wanted first of all to illustrate the greatness of Lyon's past, and to recall the importance of ancient Lugdunum in the nation's history. Inscriptions, mosaics and bronzes were added to the collection, either by donation or purchase, as and when they were found. However, the collection soon came to cover a wider field than that of Gallo-Roman artefacts. François Artaud collected Egyptian objects, which Champollion examined on numerous occasions; Artaud's

links with Bernardino Drovetti, the French consul in Alexandria, led to the gift of eight stelæ to the town in 1824.

The collection of paintings also evolved, and its utilitarian objective slowly disappeared when the École des Beaux-Arts started training young artists who became known in fields other than that of flower painting. From this time on, Lyon was not only represented by its industry but also by its artists. At the Salon of 1819, the Parisian critics used the term "Lyonnais School" for the first time, to designate the students of Pierre Révoil (1776-1842), the professor of the painting class in Lyon; these artists were highly esteemed for their genre paintings, which were done in a fine, brilliant technique. The aim of the museum soon became that of showing off the production of the School, and though these painters rapidly went out of fashion in Paris, a large part of the budget was spent on buying their works; this led to the opening, on 16 February 1851, of a "Gallery of Lyonnais Artists", with 105 items. Simultaneously, and significantly, the "Salon des Fleurs" finally disappeared in 1840.

During this period, which lasted until the 1880s, it seemed sufficient to rely on works loaned by the State to restore the balance of the collections. Although some of these works were by artists born in Lyon (Flandrin's

Dante, Led by Virgil, Puvis de Chavannes's *Autumn*), most of them were not, e.g. certain paintings (Charlet's *Episode in the Retreat from Russia*, Ziégler's *Judith*, Delacroix's *Last Words of the Emperor Marcus Aurelius*) and some very important sculptures (Barye's *Tiger*, Étex's *Cain and his Race*, Pradier's *Odalisque*, Duret's *Chactas*).

At the beginning of the last quarter of the nineteenth century, this policy showed signs of exhaustion, and a new impetus became necessary. The city authorities decided to start a restoration and enlargement project in 1878: the architect Hirsh built the main staircase, at the top of which Puvis de Chavannes installed his famous *Sacred Wood*, and which led to two vast galleries, one for the old masters and one for the modern masters. At the same time, the institution itself was overhauled, with the introduction of a board of directors, chaired for almost twenty years by a banker, politician and collector, Édouard Aynard (1837-1913). The board was made up of collectors, scholars and artists, and was given wide powers to start with, but in 1897, when the city authorities judged it to have become too independent, it was turned into a "consultative committee", mainly involved in acquisitions. However, the impetus had been given; Aynard had lucidly analysed the collections and decided on ambitious objectives, aiming at the highest level of quality. This policy was well served by a series of large donations in the form of financial trusts, which compensated in part for the small number of works donated.

And here we find another singularity of the museum: there have been no donations or bequests which, in terms of the number or quality of the works concerned, might have given the museum a particular dimension or orientation; no Wicar, Cacault or Fabre as in Lille, Nantes or Montpellier, no Lavalard as in Amiens, no Gigoux as in Besançon, no Général de Beylié as in Grenoble. Although there have been a number of donors from around Lyon — and some of these, such as Jacques-Amédée Lambert (for archæology and art objects), Jacques Bernard, Raymond Tripier, Joseph Gillet and, more recently, Léon Bouchut (for paintings), have given the museum significant collections — they bear no comparison with the prestigious examples mentioned above. On the contrary, a number of opportunities were missed, especially in the field of medieval archæology, where Lyon, in the nineteenth century, had some incomparable collections, among which were those of Révoil, acquired by the Louvre in 1828, Trimolet, given to Dijon in 1878, and Jean-Baptiste Carrand, known as the "Lyonnais museum of Cluny", which was bequeathed to Florence by his adoptive son, Louis, in 1879.

There is a point that should be particularly stressed: the museum of Lyon's collections were in large part put together, more than those of other museums, through acquisitions. This might explain their "encyclopædic" character, which is more pronounced and successful than in most other provincial museums. The collection of Italian Renaissance sculptures, with some thirty-five pieces, including the famous Sienese *Annunciation* group and Mino da Fiesole's *Saint John the Baptist*, was acquired in Florence, Venice and Rome, as well as in the great Parisian auctions, between 1880 and 1900. It was roughly at this time that Jean-Baptiste Giraud (1844-1910), the organiser and true creator of the art object department, acquired most of the Islamic collection from the Parisian auctions. In the same way, and at the same time, some very beautiful Greek and Etruscan vases and bronzes were bought. The greatest successes were achieved, however, in the domain of modern painting: in 1901, when Renoir's *Woman Playing the Guitar* was bought from Durand-Ruel, the museum of Lyon became the first outside Paris to dare put together a collection of Impressionist paintings, including at least two masterpieces, *The Café-Concert at "Les Ambassadeurs"* by Degas, and *Nave Nave Mahana* by Gauguin. The latter was, in 1913, the first of this artist's paintings to be bought by a French museum.

The acquisition policy of the museum during the period after the First World War was conducted, to a great extent, along the same lines; the means of pursuing this policy had been curtailed, however, by the devaluation of the financial trusts. The museum was directed at that time by such brilliant personalities as Henri Focillon (from 1913 to 1924), Léon

Rosenthal (from 1924 to 1933), and René Jullian (from 1933 to 1963), who maintained the "encyclopædic" orientation of the collections: Focillon was able, during the First World War, to buy the superb ceramics from the Far East collected by Raphaël Collin, while, in 1926, Rosenthal devoted a room to "modern decorative arts". Gone was the daring shown at the beginning of the century with the purchase of modern paintings: works by Bonnard, Vuillard and Fujita were bought, but the museum chose to ignore Cubist and Abstract works.

During the 1950s, René Jullian tried to make up for lost time, but he had to face hostility from the city authorities, and this made his task more difficult. He was successful, however, in buying a few important pieces; the first painting by Dubuffet to be bought by a French museum, *Blond Landscape*, was acquired by the museum of Lyon in 1956, and there were a series of gifts (Picasso in 1953, Braque and Gleizes in 1954, etc.). At the same time, the museum was finishing its appropriation of the Palais by extending into the sections that had been vacated by the École des Beaux-Arts and the Académie de Lyon.

A series of profound transformations was started in 1969, comprising the first elements of a complete reorganisation of the museum, and a redefinition of its objectives. This can be compared to what had taken place almost a century before; twenty years were needed, however, for this redefinition to take effect, and to lead to a coherent project. It was in 1969 that most of the Musée Guimet's Egyptology collections, from Adolphe Reinach's 1909-1910 excavations at Coptos, were transferred to the Palais Saint Pierre: this transfer enlarged the scope of the department of Antiquities, which was severely diminished by the simultaneous transfer of Gallo-Roman objects to the museum of Fourvière. It was thus necessary to imagine a new presentation of these archæological collections, which were made up for the most part of large stones. Furthermore, the

museum's relations with modern and contemporary art needed more radical changes than the "catching up" activity of the previous decades: a contemporary art section was created in 1984 in the so-called "New Saint Pierre" wing; it became autonomous almost immediately, and rapidly developed. Finally, the fact that large numbers of works were piled up in the reserves because of the lack of exhibition space and the dilapidated state of certain parts of the buildings, as well as the almost complete absence of modern amenities for the public, meant that a restoration and extension of the museum had become indispensable.

The decision was taken in 1989; it was due to the willingness and financial means of both the State — as part of the Ministry of Culture's "Grands Travaux" programme — and the city of Lyon. A brief recapitulation of what it entailed might be useful here. The only available space for extension was that of the New Saint Pierre, i.e. 4,500 m2 on four levels; this meant that the museum of contemporary art had to be given a new site, and that the Beaux-Arts museum's collections no longer covered art produced after 1960. This development has now been completed, and the contemporary art collections have been rehoused in a new building on the Quai Achille Lignon.

The remodelling of the Palais Saint Pierre, which started in 1990, was put in the hands of the architects Philippe Charles Dubois and Jean-Michel

Wilmotte; the work was divided into five stages (subsequently eight, for financial reasons). The reorganisation of the collections entailed moving three departments to the first floor (Antiquities, Art Objects, Graphic Arts Cabinet), putting all the paintings, including those of the Lyonnais School, on the second floor, where ceiling lighting was installed, placing the sculptures and larger paintings in the Chapel, and, finally, creating temporary exhibition spaces in the New Saint Pierre, as well as installing visitors' amenities and reception spaces on the ground floor, and on the first floor of the South wing.

As I write these lines (summer 1995), over half the programme has been completed, and it is due to be finished by the beginning of 1998. The restoration of the museum's entire 14,500 m2, with its 70 rooms, will

provide an extraordinary journey through Western civilisation, from Pharaonic Egypt to Picasso. This perfectly ordered diversity will, I believe, give us a tremendous asset, with its human dimensions and the intimate harmony of the site. I trust that it will enable one of the most beautiful of French museums to begin its third century of existence in the most favourable conditions.

1
Henri Focillon, *Le Musée de Lyon, peintures*, Paris, H. Laurens, 1919, Memoranda, p. 6.
2
Ibid.

3
Report of 3 March 1799, cf. M.C. Chaudonneret, "Les origines du musée des Beaux-Arts de Lyon. 1791-1799", *Bulletin des musées et monuments lyonnais*, 1986, vol. VII, n° 1, p. 79-95.

Antiquities
Rooms 1 to 16

Egypt
End of the Old Kingdom /
First Intermediate
Period (c. 2150-2040 B.C.)

Coffin of Teti-Anu
Polychrome wood
L. 1.76; W. 0.38; H. 0.49
Entered the collection in 1969
Inv. 1972-114

This fine coffin, which was discovered during R. Weill's excavations in Assiut, in Middle Egypt, is composed of a rectangular trough with a wooden lid, decorated with rows and columns of blue-painted hieroglyphic text. The inscriptions which run along the exterior of the sides, the angles, and the edge of the trough, are devoted to the four sons of Horus (Hapi, Amset, Duamutef and Qebehsenuf), and to the four children of Atum (Shu, Tefnut, Geb and Nut). Two udjat-eyes are painted on the eastern side of the receptacle so as to allow the dead person, who had to be laid on his left side, to look at the bank of the Nile over which the sun rises. The panel corresponding to the head is placed under the protection of Nepthys and Neith, that of the feet under the protection of Isis and Selkis. The inscriptions on the cover are devoted to Anubis and Nut. The interior of the coffin is painted plain yellow.

The museum possesses four examples of this type of coffin, which is characteristic of the Middle Kingdom.

V.G./J.C.G.

Egypt
XXIIth to XVth Dynasty
(c. 945-712 B.C.)

Interior of the Trough and
Lid of the Coffin of Istemkheb
Stuccoed and painted
polychrome wood
L. 1.76; W. 0.48; H. 0.43
Entered the collection in 1969
Inv. 1969-197

During the New Kingdom, sarcophagi began to adopt an anthropomorphic form, as is illustrated by that of Istemkheb, daughter of Ankhsyeniset.

In the inside of the cover, the theme represented is that of the solarisation of the deceased. It represents Nut, who is dressed in a red reticulated robe which accentuates her starred body. Her arms, raised above her head, are holding the sun, which she swallows each evening in the west and brings back into the world each morning in the east. The dead person, identified with Rêᶜ, is thus placed inside the body of the goddess, who ensures her protection and regeneration. The interior of the receptacle is devoted to the rebirth of Osiris. An image of the djed-pillar, which is a symbol of the spine of Osiris and is endowed with the attributes of the mummy-shaped god of Abydos, is painted at the spot where the dead person's back would be. The erection of this pillar in the towns of Busiris and Letopolis marked the triumph of Osiris over death. During the evocation of this episode, Osiris would draw the mummy along with him, placing it in an upright position so as to favour its resurrection. Thus protected, the mummy would benefit fully from the destinies of the sun and of Osiris, which were the only guarantees of eternal life.
V.G./J.C.G.

Anthropomorphic figurines (pages 21, 22), which began to be known as "ushabtis" in the New Kingdom, were placed in tombs to act as substitutes for the mummies, whose appearance they took on. They replaced the dead person in the duties he was supposed to take up in the afterlife.

Egypt
XIXth Dynasty
(c. 1307-1196 B.C.)

Bakenkhonsu's Ushabti
Painted sycamore wood
H. 0.244; W. 0.051; Th. 0.038
Loaned by The State, 1893
Inv. E 313

This painted wooden ushabti from the tomb of Bakenkhonsu is wrapped in a mummy-shaped sheath inscribed with the name and sacerdotal title of the dead person, and an unfinished version of Chapter 6 of the *Book of the Dead*. His arms are crossed on his breast, and in each hand he holds a painted ploughing implement, recalling the agricultural work that there is to be done. At the age of 64, during the reign of Ramses II, Bakenkhonsu held the highest religious rank in the state, that of first prophet of Amun. His tomb was discovered in the region of west Thebes, at Dra abul'Naga.
V.G./J.C.G.

**Third Intermediate Period
(c. 1070-712 B.C.)**

Amenhotep's Ushabti
Blue faience with black highlights
H. 0.131; W. 0.041; Th. 0.023
Gift of Bernardino Drovetti, 1835
Inv. A 2526

The period of weakening of the royal power which followed the New Kingdom had an effect on the production of ushabtis, which went into decline. Henceforth they were moulded and produced in large numbers, and the inscription was reduced to a simple statement of the dead person's name, written lengthwise on the legs. The inscription on this ushabti informs us that Amenhotep was the "Father of God, beloved by God, supreme purifier of the temple, first of the sacerdotal scribes in the domain of Amun". V.G./J.C.G.

**Late Period
(c. 712-332 B.C.)**

Saiset's Ushabti
Green enamelled frit
H. 0.160; W. 0.041; Th. 0.023
Acquired in 1835
Inv. A 2531

Saiset's ushabti is typical of the funerary figurines which appeared with the coming to power of the Saïte Dynasty. The ushabtis of this period began to be placed on stands, leaning against a dorsal pillar. The text inscribed on the mummy-shaped sheath informs us that Saiset held the sacerdotal title of "he who separates the two gods"; this priestly function was specific to the region of Mendes, east of the Nile delta. V.G./J.C.G.

Egypt
XIIth Dynasty
(c. 1971-1926 B.C.)

Fragment of the Lintel
of Serwosret (Sesostris) I
Limestone
H. 1.46; L. 1.00
Entered the collection in 1969
Inv. E 501

This lintel was found in 1909 by A. Reinach among re-used building materials in the foundations of the Roman gate close to the "central" edifice in Koptos, along with ten large limestone blocks and a considerable number of fragments. These all came from the monumental gate which, in the Middle Kingdom, marked the main entrance to the great temple dedicated to Min, which was one of the most important sanctuaries of Upper Egypt during that period.

As was shown by the restoration work and studies that were carried out in 1988, this block, which comes from the left face of the inner lintel of the gate, represents a "royal ascent" towards the goddess Wadjet, who is located on the right. The king, of whom one sees only the right hand, is being led by a falcon-headed figure evoking the city of Pê (Buto) in the delta. Under the right shoulder of the figure there is a graffito suggesting an obelisk.
V.G./J.C.G.

Egypt
Reigns of Ptolemy III and IV
(c. 246-205 B.C.)

Gates of Medamud
Polychrome sandstone
H. 3.80; W. 5.20; Th. 3.00
Gift of the Institut Français
d'Archéologie Orientale, 1939
Inv. 1939-29

Two monumental gates were found among re-used building materials in the foundations of a late monument at the temple of Montu in Medamud, to the north of Luxor. Ptolemy IV's gate is the more recent of the two, and the most complete. It most probably stood in the axis of the main temple of Medamud, in an intercolumnar space. On the shafts of the pillars, the Pharaoh is seen holding the sceptre of consecration and the ceremonial stick, and his gesture is that which generally accompanies a liturgical formula for the presentation of an offering. He is advancing through the interior of the gate towards the "Great Imposing Bull Montu". On the right-hand shaft, he officiates for the south, wearing a white crown; on the left, the gesture is repeated for the north, and the sovereign is wearing a red crown. The door-frame is simply decorated with friezes of monumental signs. As to the reverse side, it is incomplete. On the right, the king is portrayed receiving a sword and a mekes-case from the hands of Amun.

The second door, that of Ptolemy III, is more fragmentary, and is decorated on the shafts with three superimposed registers of scenes where offerings are being made to the local manifestations of the divinity and to their Theban equivalents. On the external lintel, the king is participating in a rowing race and a helm race in the monarchic jubilee ritual.

This gate probably allowed access to the sacrifice chamber in the temple, given its decorative programme of food offerings.

V.G./J.C.G.

Egypt
Roman period
(end of the 1st century B.C.)

Bas-relief: *Cæsarion*
Making Offerings
Limestone
H. 0.44; W. 1.33; Th. 0.15
Entered the collection in 1969
Inv. E 501

This block, which originally came from the temple of Koptos, was discovered by A. Reinach in 1911, along with several others which are on show in the museum, in the remains of a church and baptistery to the west of Koptos. It represents, on the right, a Pharaoh wearing a short wig clasped by a diadem with a frontal uræus, offering fabrics and unguent to two unidentified deities. The god is either Harpocrates (Horus the child) holding the "heka" and the flagellum, or else Khonsu. As to the goddess, she may be Isis, the "paredra" of Min at Koptos, or perhaps Mut, the mother of Khonsu.

Reinach dated this block, in the context of the find, to the period of Cleopatra VII and Cæsarion. This datation seems quite plausible, if one compares it to that of other reliefs which are known to date from the end of the Ptolemaic domination. The modelling of the faces is perfectly executed, evoking the characteristic style of the Ptolemies, but the absence of inscriptions, as well as the incompleteness of the treatment of the divine figures on the left, might be taken to correspond to the period which saw the intervention of Octavian in Egypt, when the monuments dedicated to the last Ptolemaic sovereigns were abandoned.
V.G./J.C.G.

Egypt
Reign of Ptolemy II and
Arsinoe I
(c. 285-246 B.C.)

Stand for Boat or Statue
Pink granite
H. 1.15; W. 0.73; Th. 0.92
Entered the collection in 1969
Inv. E 501

This stand for a divine boat (or statue), dating from the period of Ptolemy II and Arsinoe I, was discovered in re-used building materials from a Coptic church to the west of Koptos, which was excavated in 1910-1911 by A. Reinach. Worked in pink granite, it has been given the form which was traditional for Egyptian gates and pylons, topped with a grooved cornice engraved with palmettes. Only the front face is decorated, with a winged disc above a vertical column of hieroglyphic text which reads: "The king of Upper and Lower Egypt, Woser-ka-Rê^c, beloved of Amun, son of Rê^c, lord of the crowns, Ptolemy, beloved of Khonsu the Plan-maker of Thebes, the great god who cuts down enemies and saves his Majesty in the 'Duat', and is endowed, like Rê^c, with life forever", and "The daughter of Amun Arsinoe, the goddess Philadelphe".
This dedication, which is typically Theban, dates from after 270 HB.C., which would lead one to suspect that there may have existed in Koptos an edifice devoted to the Theban divinities, or else that this monument was taken to Koptos from one of the sanctuaries of Karnak.
V.G./J.C.G.

Egypt
Reign of Amenhotep II,
XVIIIth Dynasty
(c. 1427-1401 B.C.)

Scarab of Amenhotep II
Enamelled stone
L. 0.050; W. 0.035; H. 0.020
Loaned by the Institut d'Égyptologie
V. Loret, Lyon, 1991
Inv. I.E. 127 A.F.

The scarab is an image of existence manifesting itself; as black or blue as the night within which it is plunged, it can represent the sun bursting through over the horizon. There were large scarabs in stone or faience that were intended to serve as substitutes for the heart of the dead person, in which case they were worn on necklaces, or else placed where the heart would be, inside the thorax, during the final stage of embalming.

The scarabs in this category, which were individualised, often bore inscriptions from the *Book of the Dead*, so that the heart, identified with the scarab, should not be opposed to it in the empire of the dead. There are other specimens which have no funerary purpose; they form another category, called "commemorative", which was at times widely disseminated, in the manner of postage stamps; some served as ex-libris, attached to the fixations that closed the rolls of papyrus in the Pharaonic libraries. This example incorporates, on its flat side, under a winged disc, an engraved inscription of five lines which recalls the domination of Pharaoh Amenhotep II on the borders of the Egyptian kingdom: in the north-west, towards Mitanni (modern-day Iraq), and in the south, the territory of Kush (Sudan) — "The perfect god, sovereign of Thebes, lord of the Two Lands, Aa-kheperu-Rêc (Amenhotep II), the victorious arm with the sword that despoils the chiefs of Naharina, the victorious-armed who tramples underfoot the vile land of Kush, and is gifted with eternal life".

This scarab may have served to seal the "volumen" of the royal annals which deals with the Asian campaigns of the years 7 and 9 of the reign of Amenhotep II, at the end of which a Syrian prince, an ally of the Mitannians, was hanged on the ramparts of the town of Napata, in the land of Kush, as an example.
V.G./J.C.G.

Egypt
XXVIth to XXXth Dynasties
(664-343 B.C.)

The Nile God Hapi
Bronze
H. 0.208; L. 0,050; Depth 0,073
Acquired in 1835
Inv. H 1517

Hapi was the divine name for the overflowing of the river Nile; this statuette personifies him as a being of marked corpulence, bringing the benefits of the flood in the form of offerings. On his head is a triple sheaf of plants from the marshes of the north. The broken-off hands would probably have held a plate of victuals, the products of the earth. The rectangular base is inscribed with a dedicatory formula: "May Hapi grant life to Tjahapyimu, the son of Ptahirdisu..."

In Egypt, the waters of the flood of Hapi are linked to the idea of luxuriance and fecundity, and represent a promise of miraculous fertility.

Bronze statuettes of the god Hapi are very rare, and the example seen here is the only one of this quality that is known of; it is also among the most ancient specimens of Egyptian art to have been brought to France. Before coming to the museum, it belonged to the collection of President F.X. Bon de Saint Hilaire in Montpellier, in 1761, then to that of Count de Caylus (or perhaps Count de Migieu).

V.G./J.C.G.

Egypt
Old Kingdom, IVth Dynasty
(c. 2575-2465 B.C.)

Anonymous Couple
Polychrome limestone
H. 0.365; L. 0,23; Depth 0,19
Inv. H 1724

This anepigraphic statuary group belongs to the sculptural tradition of the Old Kingdom. The man is standing on the right, with his wife on his left. He is wearing a short loincloth and a wig with several rows of tight curls. His wife is wearing a dress which reaches down to her ankles, and her half-length hair frames her face symmetrically. The general bearing of the bodies, which is without any great distinction, contrasts with the treatment of the faces, which are rendered in a way which suggests that the artist was seeking to give them the value of portraits.

Family groups of this kind, which above all show the Egyptian attachment to the family unit, were originally placed in the "serdab", a niche set aside in the chapel on top of the mastaba, to recall the memory of dead members of the family. These statues played the role of substitutes, and were considered as being alive, receiving visits and offerings during the ceremonies of the funerary cult.

V.G./J.C.G.

Egypt
Middle Kingdom, XIIth
Dynasty (c. 1991-1783 B.C.)

Model: *The Audience with*
the Lord-A
Polychrome wood
L. 0.29; W. 0.28
Entered the collection in 1969
Inv. 1969-404

Wooden models appeared in Egypt at the end of the Old Kingdom, and subsequently proliferated. They reproduced scenes from everyday life. Placed in tombs, they gave the dead person access to maids, servants and artisans to accompany him or her into the afterlife and to carry out the necessary chores of life.

This model, which was probably unearthed in 1913 during R. Weill's excavations in Assiut, portrays an audience devoted to an account of activities. In an open court, the lord is seated with his hands on his knees, listening to the reports and grievances of his six servants, who are gathered together in front of him. Some of them are bowing humbly, others are leaning on sticks, and one is carrying a sack.

This scene, with the dead person taking pleasure in recalling his authority, is an evocation of a daily routine, but also expresses the dead person's wish to see his family and household assembled around him, to carry out in his presence the agricultural tasks involved in the afterlife. This role of substitute was taken on, in the New Kingdom and afterwards, by the ushabti.

V.G./J.C.G.

Egypt
Reign of Amenhotep III,
XVIIIth Dynasty
(c. 1391-1353 B.C.)

Stela of Ptahmes
Polychrome limestone
H. 0.86; W. 0.56; Th. 0.12
Gift of Bernardino Drovetti, 1824
Inv. H 1376

This stela was presented to the city of Lyon by the great Egyptologist Bernardino Drovetti; it was most probably brought from the region of Abydos by Jean-Jacques Rifaud, where it was found in a votive chapel dedicated to Osiris by the family of the high dignitary Ptahmes.

In the rounded upper part of the stela, under a winged disc which protects the cartouche of Amenhotep III, Ptahmes, "First Prophet of Amun, Vizier of Thebes, Director of all the Works", is performing a double adoration to Osiris, who is placed in the centre, under a dais. Ptahmes is dressed in the vizier's long robe and the sacerdotal feline skin. Before him are three offering-tables laden with victuals, flowers and vases. The middle section depicts, on the left, Ptahmes and his wife Ipeny, seated, receiving a tribute of flowers from their two sons and five daughters. The lower section is occupied by ten lines of finely engraved text. In a hymn to the universality of the divine powers, the author evokes the rectitude and terrestrial excellence of Ptahmes in the service of the state and of his sovereign Amenhotep III. At the end of the prayer, the last sentences ask visitors to join in the act of piety of Amun's prophet, and to imitate his irreproachable conduct.

V.G./J.C.G.

Egypt
End of the XVIIIth Dynasty
(c. 1427-1323 B.C.)

Head of a Man
Inlaid wood
H. 0.089; W. 0.056; Th. 0.057
Gift of Bernardino Drovetti, 1835
Inv. H 1368

Delicately sculpted in a dark wood resembling ebony, this head of a young man is of unknown origin and attribution. It has a square tenon, and may have been the terminal part of the base of a harp, based on a design that was in vogue at the end of the XVIIIth Dynasty. The juvenile face is thick-lipped, with eyes which are drawn back markedly towards the temples, and which were formerly inlaid with stones imitating the iris and cornea; the figure is wearing a short wig with wavy locks whose ends are held in clips in the form of double pearls.

This exceptional piece has been compared to a figure in faience, now in the Louvre, whose somewhat melancholy expression is similar to this one. Both may be dated to the very end of the XVIIIth Dynasty, Tutankhamen's time, though it is not absolutely impossible that this piece belongs to the reign of Amenhotep III, before the Amarna episode.

V.G./J.C.G.

Egypt
XVIIIth Dynasty
(c. 1550-1070 B.C.)

Make-up Spoon in the form
of a Hobbled Oryx
Bone
L. 0.085; W. 0.025
Loaned by the Institut d'Égyptologie
V. Loret, Lyon, 1988
Inv. I.E. 512

The animal, which is not wearing a collar around its neck, is tightly tied, with its legs folded under its belly, and is turned towards the right. Its open mouth suggests its call of distress at the sight of approaching death.

This theme was frequently used for toilet items during the XVIIIth Dynasty, in the reign of Amenhotep III and his immediate successors. The bowl of the spoon, which is concealed on its reverse side by the belly of the animal, was meant for an unguent, probably a cosmetic most often used for decorating the rims of the eyes, while also having a protective function. The cosmetic was prepared from powdered galena (lead sulphide) or chrysocolla (copper sulphate) amalgamated with an oily substance to give black and green varieties. Such cosmetics and unguents were in daily use, like the recipients and utensils that served for their preparation; they were among the favourite toilet articles of the dead, and examples dating from all periods have been found among the paraphernalia required for the Other World.

V.G./J.C.G.

Egypt
Roman Period
(2nd-3rd centuries A.D.)

Stela of a Palmyrene
of Koptos
Polychrome sandstone
H. 0.72; W. 0.49
Entered the collection in 1969
Inv. E 501

A set of twelve stelæ of this type were unearthed in 1911 by A. Reinach at Koptos, in what he called the "house of the Palmyrenes". This building seems to have been the meeting-place of a corporation of archers and merchants from Palmyra, living in Koptos. Seven of these stelæ are in the Museum of Fine Arts, the others in the museum of Cairo. The iconography is identical for all these pieces. Two male figures are represented side by side, holding either an arrow or a "mappa", a sort of schematic garland. They are set in a "naos" above which is a frieze with upright uræi crowned with the solar disc, a typically Egyptian motif, like the grooved cornice and the torus above which the frieze of cobras reigns.

The centre of the building where the stelæ were found was occupied by two altars, which seems to indicate its function as the chapel of a confraternity where religious acts were performed.

Koptos was situated in Upper Egypt, at the starting point of the roads leading to the Red Sea. In the Ptolemaic era the city was on the main route for commercial exchanges with the south, and had an active community of merchants from all round the Mediterranean, including some from Palmyra.
V.G./J.C.G.

Egypt
Coptic Period
(4th-5th centuries A.D.)

Bas-relief with Dove
Limestone
H. 0.88; W. 0.52; Th. 0.08
Entered the collection in 1969
Inv. E 501

This bas-relief, which comes from a Coptic church, or baptistery, situated to the west of the site of Koptos, was discovered in 1911 during A. Reinach's excavations. It was a component either of an ambo or an iconostasis, and represents, in its central part, a dove (or perhaps a hoopoe) with outspread wings — a symbol of peace — above which are four intertwined crosses.

The rest of the surface is occupied by a frieze of foliage with cruciform flowers. This intertwined pattern is framed by a second foliage motif. In this bas-relief, the sculptor clearly asserts his refusal of Pharaonic and Hellenistic art, from which Coptic art was nonetheless directly derived. He has preferred the choice of a floral, animal décor, based essentially on abstraction, of a kind which was subsequently to be a direct source of inspiration to Muslim artists.

V.G./J.C.G.

Egypt
Coptic Period
(4th-5th centuries A.D.)

Patera
Bronze
L. 0.330; Diam. 0.175
Loaned by the Institut d'Égyptologie
V. Loret, Lyon, 1988
Inv. I.E.C. 8

This cupule-shaped recipient forming a dipper for sacral water (whose technical name is "patera") is provided with a remarkable handle which is strongly pagan in inspiration. It features, in effect, a young woman who is totally naked except for a sort of thick necklace with an ampulla-shaped pendant. She is standing upright with her legs crossed. Her arms, with heavy bracelets round her wrists, are raised above her head, and are holding up a double garland of palms enclosing the eastern Christian cross, the "Coptic cross". Two umbilicate spheres are leaning against her knees, and are held in place, on either side, by the arced tails of two open-mouthed monsters spitting ball-shaped objects. These monstrous animals have crocodile bodies, and are crawling on their bellies; their heads are heavily accentuated, and curved scorpions' tails are grafted onto the middle of their backs.

This object is exceptional, if not unique, in the current state of knowledge. It takes up, and adapts, two related themes from the iconography of Egyptian magic: Hathor-Anat, naked, standing on maleficent animals (the heavy necklace worn by the figure on the patera recalls the goddess's "menat" necklace), and Horus "on the crocodiles", which was much in vogue at the end of the Pharaonic era. These tutelary forms of the divinity figured on stelæ and amulets. These were sprinkled with, and plunged into, water which was said to possess curative and preventive virtues, and to give protection against dangerous or venomous beings. In Christianised form, such practices were perpetuated beyond the 3rd century, but with holy water, as this ceremonial cup demonstrates.
V.G./J.C.G.

Assyria
Nimrud, third quarter of the
8th century B.C.

Head of Priest
Gypseous alabaster
H. 0.55; W. 0.43; Th. 0.08
Exchanged with the Musée d'Arles
in 1936
Inv. 1936-60

The sculpture, which was found at Nimrud in 1852, illustrates the enthusiasm occasioned in the 19th century by the first discoveries made in Mesopotamia, and the birth of Assyriology.

This fragment from a bas-relief represents a masculine head in profile, with a voluminous curly beard and finely-braided hair held in a rosette-decorated net, the ears adorned by rings with pendants. It is thought to have come from the "gallery of what is known as Sardanapalus's palace". It was first presented to the town of Arles by the owner of a stud farm on his return from Asia Minor, and in 1936 arrived in the Museum of Fine Arts in exchange for an Arlesian coffin. It probably comes from the palace of Tiglath-Pileser III at Nimrud (formerly Kalakh), a monumental site comprising the palaces of several Assyrian kings which was partially explored by the English archaeologist Sir Austen Henry Layard. One of these palaces, built by Shalmaneser III (858-824 B.C.) and restored by Tiglath-Pileser III (744-727 B.C.), had no sooner been brought to light than it yielded up a large quantity of reliefs, winged lions and bulls which, for the most part, went to the British Museum. The complete figure, as drawn by Layard, shows that the man was wearing a garment decorated with fringes and borders of rosettes alternating with squares. His lowered left arm was holding a branch with three flowers, his right being raised in a sign of prayer or homage. This would indicate that the piece represents a priest participating in a ritual ceremony linked to the power of the Assyrian king.

G.G.

Persepolis
5th century B.C.

Water-skin Carrier
Stone
H. 0.430; W. 0.300; Th. 0.105
Acquired in 1932
Inv. B 1701

This fragment of a bas-relief was bought by the museum in 1932. It was taken to be from the "palace of Persepolis", the new capital built by Darius in his native country, Fars, to exalt the power of the Achæmenid dynasty, and which contained the finest edifices that Persia had seen up to that time, notably the palace of Darius and that of his son Xerxes, in which, each spring, was held the great feast of the god Ahura-mazda, during which all the nations of the empire laid offerings at the foot of the throne of the king of kings in token of submission. Wall reliefs celebrated the high points of the ceremony; for example, the monumental staircases leading to the banqueting hall were decorated with servants climbing the steps, laden down with dishes, and animals intended to be served up at the tables. It was from such a processional scene that this water-skin carrier would very likely have come. The man, seen in profile, stands out against an empty background, in keeping with the techniques of Achæmenid monumental art. He is moving towards the right, his two hands supporting a skin filled with water or wine which is resting on his shoulder. The veil around his head and chin reveals a profile with large almond-shaped eyes, a hooked nose and a small fringe of curls.

G.G.

Cyprus
Late 4th century-3rd
century B.C.

Veiled Head of a Woman
White limestone
H. 0.120; W. 0.088; Th. 0.085
Acquired in 1896
Inv. E 366

This fine head in limestone is a portrait of a young girl; it was acquired from a merchant in Constantinople in 1896 among an assortment of antiquarian pieces from Cyprus.

The young Cypriot is turning her head imperceptibly towards the right, as is indicated by the fold in the neck and the direction of the look, which can be discerned despite the almost complete disappearance of colour from the pupils. The face, which is perfectly modelled, is accentuated by the sharply-defined bridge of the nose and the arch of the eyebrows, as well as the slight smile that plays round the mouth, with its finely drawn lips. A simple veil placed on the back of the head falls elegantly on either side of the face, revealing a pair of ear-rings, while the hair, separated at the front into locks, is twisted round a band.

This sculpture, which is of very high quality, is representative of Cypriot art at the start of the Hellenistic period, when Greek art had already left a deep influence on the island, and the originality of its art was disappearing little by little under the domination of the Ptolemies. This head is of remarkable size by comparison with the miniaturist pieces of the period, and in all likelihood belongs to the type of statues of veiled women inspired by Greek funerary art and propagated by Tanagra terracotta figurines, which frequently served as models for votive representations of women in Cyprus during the 4th century B.C. and thereafter.

G.G.

**Syria,
Palmyra, 121 A.D.**

*Bas-relief with the Gods Bel,
Baal-shamin, Yarhi-bol and
Agli-bol*
Limestone
L. 0.54; H. 0.45
Acquired in 1992
Inv. 1992-13

This bas-relief represents four divine figures, of whom two are standing, with another seated on each side, the group as a whole being set in a frame that has been partly eroded. Below, there is a cartouche containing an inscription in the Palmyrene language, which was a variant of Aramaic: "These images figuring Bel, Baal-shamin, Yarhi-bol and Agli-bol were made by Ba'alay, son of Yedi'bel, son of Ba'alay, in the month of Tebet, in the year 432". This dedication puts the two supreme gods of the Palmyrene pantheon first, followed by the two ancillary divinities. The inscription ends in the habitual way, with the date, namely 121 A.D. according to the calendar used at Palmyra, i.e. that of the Seleucids, which began in 311 B.C.

The originality of the monument derives from the way in which it represents the four divinities. The supreme gods Bel and Baal-shamin are treated in exactly symmetrical manner. In this case Bel, who in general is shown beardless, has a beard and hair. He is wearing a *calathos* with floating bands, and a tunic under his armour. An ample cloak passes over his shoulder and envelops his legs. Baal-shamin is draped in a Greek-style garment. The two central divinities, clad in armour and radiant, are undifferentiated except by Yarhi-bol's crescent moon. The scene is completed by two animals: a gryphon and a bull, the symbol of fertility. Compared to the bas-reliefs of the Palmyrene region, the high quality of the sculpting in this case, as well as the care taken in the composition, and the clear influence of Greco-Roman motifs, suggest that the piece was made in Palmyra itself. Also in evidence here is the process of assimilation of local divinities to the Greek pantheon.
G.G.

Greece
c. 540-530 B.C.

Kore
Marble
H. 0.63; W. 0.34
Entered the collection between
1808 and 1814
Inv. H 1993

In 1935, an English archæologist had the idea of putting together some fragments of a left shoulder and draped legs, found on the Acropolis in Athens, with a bust in the Museum of Fine Arts, thus giving back its identity to a kore which, from the first time it was mentioned in Gravier's collection in Marseille, in 1719, up to its acquisition by the curator François Artaud at the start of the 19th century, was successively identified as Minerva, Isis, and Aphrodite with a dove. The kore is an image of a young Athenian girl presented to the goddess Athena, and, with the kouros, is the epitome of archaic Greek sculpture. The model is represented in an upright position, facing forward. Her left arm, which has disappeared, would have followed the line of her body; her right arm is bent over her abdomen, and she is holding a bird in her hand. She is dressed in the Ionian fashion; as well as a *chiton* (i.e. a fine, clinging, long-sleeved tunic) with a decoration, barely engraved, which suggests embroidery, she is wearing a *himation* (a woollen cloak fastened at the shoulder) which drapes her elegantly. On her head she is wearing a *polos* decorated with engraved garlands which have retained traces of polychromy. Her wavy hair falls over her forehead in three long tresses on either side of her face, and covers her back in a wide swathe which is cut up into a regular pattern of small squares. Her ear-rings, which have been sculpted directly in the marble, are particularly refined. The roundness of the modelling, the softness of the face and the fineness of the composition attenuate the massive aspect of the sculpture. The particular style of this kore, which sets it slightly apart from ancient Athenian works of the archaic period, explains the uncertainty which persisted for a considerable time as to its origin. In effect, the sculptor has worked "in the Ionian style" on a purely Attic type of structure, but has retained nothing of his oriental models except their external characteristics, i.e. the clothing and the forms of certain facial features. In this respect, the kore shown here is an excellent example of the influence of foreign artists on the Attic sculpture of the archaic period.
G.G.

Greece
c. 2300-2000 B.C.

Kernos from the Cyclades
Painted earthenware with slip
H. 0.35; Diam. 0.34
Acquired in 1859
Inv. X 282

In the third millennium B.C., the Cyclades, small islands in the middle of the Ægean sea, experienced an extraordinary period of development. At the start of the Bronze Age a civilisation known essentially from its funerary objects elaborated a flourishing culture which expressed itself notably in the arts of metallurgy, marble-working and pottery. This kernos, which was found in Athens, is typical, in its shape and painted décor, of the production of the end of this period (Late Cycladic III). The vase is made up of several small cups in terracotta, individually modelled and joined together, without intercommunication, by rolls of clay. Thirteen oblong recipients form an external ring, surrounding a composition of three small cups alternating with three others, which are broader and lower. The crown thus formed rests on a high cylindrical foot, which is splayed out at the base. The red clay, containing particles of a sandy scouring agent, is covered in a white slip decorated with black vertical and crossed lines. The kernos is considered as a vessel with a ritual function.
G.G.

Greece
First half of the 6th century B.C.

Painted Amphora
Black-figure ceramic
H. 0.300; Diam. 0.215
Loaned by the State, 1863
Inv. X 482-68

This Attic amphora comes from the famed collection of Marquis Campana, which was acquired by Napoleon III in 1861. An amphora — a vase intended for transporting and containing liquids and other commodities — is said to be "à tableau" when the line of the neck continues without interruption over the belly and the decoration is incorporated into a panel reserved in the glaze. This particular amphora features the black-figure technique, the painted motifs standing out against the light background of the ceramic; it is adorned on each side with a horse protome. The details of the animal figure — the ear, eye, nostril, the elements of the harness and the fine locks of the mane — are brought out in dark red and out lined by incisions in the glaze.

The repetitive character of the decoration, and its sobriety, suggest that this type of "horse-head" amphora, produced in Athens during the first half of the 6th century B.C., may have been a prize awarded to the winner of a horse race; this would make it the ancestor of the panathenæan amphorae, containing oil from the sacred olive trees, which were presented to the winners of sports contests during the Panathenæa, the Athenian festival.

G.G.

Greece
First half of the 5th century B.C.

Mirror with Stand
Bronze
H. 0.395; Diam. disc 0.175
Acquired in 1884
Inv. E 152 5

This fine mirror on a stand, which was discovered at Corinth, evokes the Greek woman's liking for items of toiletry and adornment.

The disc which constitutes the mirror properly speaking is bordered by a double row of ova and pearls, and its stand, which is cut in whorls, is decorated with elegant incised foliage. The back of the base is decorated with a palmette in relief. The shaft is formed by a figurine of Aphrodite, the goddess of love and beauty, wearing a peplos held at the shoulder by two hooks, and which she is drawing up with her left hand, while her outstretched right hand is holding a flower. She has a band of pearls on her head, and her wavy hair is knotted behind, falling down her back. The axis of the figure is slightly out of line with the disc: the head suggests a movement towards the right, while the hip and the left shoulder are drawn back markedly. This movement of the body fits in with the stylistic current adopted around 480 B.C., which, refusing the rigidity of frontality, developed a taste for torsions which liberated the folds of garments. The two Eros figures flying around Aphrodite complete the figurative décor. The goddess's feet are resting on a circular base mounted with pearls; this allowed the mirror to be free-standing.

This particular mirror came, in all likelihood, from a workshop in Sicyone, in the Peloponnese. The quality and refinement of the execution illustrate perfectly the art of the bronze workers in Greek antiquity.

G.G.

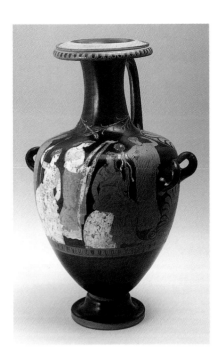

Greece
Second quarter
of the 4th century B.C.

Hydria
Polychrome Attic ceramic
H. 0.465; Diam. 0.255
Acquired in 1898
Inv. E 388-a

The hydria (the word is derived from the Greek word for water) is a pitcher with three handles, one vertical and two horizontal; it was used for fetching and containing water. This hydria belongs to what is known as the "Kerch" style, from the name of a site in Crimea, on the Black Sea, where several such vases, made in Athens, were found; it is marked by the use of a broad palette of colours, on a ceramic background with red figures. In this work, the artist reveals a great mastery of space and volumes. The range of colours used — pink, green, grey, and the white of the carnations, brought out in gold in slight relief — gives a remarkable intensity to the representation. The vase has been given a black glaze with metallescent highlights. It is decorated, on one side, with a figurative scene. In the centre of the composition, Demeter, seated with a sceptre in her hand, is turning towards her daughter Prosperine, who is descending towards her, a torch in each hand. On the left there is Triptolemus, and a woman playing a tambourine. On the right, Dionysus is sitting on the *omphalos*, his head turned towards the two goddesses, holding the pine-cone-tipped thyrsus; behind him there is a female dancer. The décor of the vase is completed by a crown of myrtle around its neck, and palmettes grouped together on the handles. The scene is drawn from the Eleusinian mysteries: the worship of the three divinities there involved rites about which little is known due to the fact that the members of the sect were not allowed to reveal anything about their initiation; it is, however, known that the cult was linked to fecundity, and to the hope of survival after death. This hydria, found in 1883 in a grave in a necropolis of ancient Capua — which would explain the funerary character of the representation — is a sign of the development of the exchanges which took place between Athens and Magna Græcia at that time.
G.G.

Roman Empire
1st century A.D.

Mercury
Bronze
H. 0.230; W. 0.071
Jacques-Amédée Lambert Bequest, 1850
Inv. L 217

Mercury, son of Jupiter, is one of the twelve Olympian gods, and is their messenger. Identified with the Greek god Hermes, he protects, in particular, merchants and voyagers. His representation, under different aspects, was common in the Roman period.

Here, the god is seen standing up, naked, his head tilted slightly towards the left. His face, whose realistic features suggest certain portraits of the Flavian period, is lit up by the gleam of the eyes, which are inlaid with silver. Between the fine curls of his hair appear the points of attachment of wings which have been broken off, but which allow his identity to be determined. The arms have also disappeared, but it may be supposed that the figure was holding an attribute. The figure is leaning on his right leg, with the left being thrown sharply backwards, produces a marked twisting effect, which brings out an anatomy with powerful, elegant proportions. In the treatment of the body at rest, whose clearly-expressed musculature nonetheless gives it the impression of being in movement, the artist was directly inspired by classical Greek statuary, and in particular by the great sculptor Lysippos; this influence sets the work apart from the serial production of the period.
G.G.

Roman Empire
Middle of the 3rd century A.D.

Head of a Roman Woman
Marble
H. 0.25; W. 0.16
Acquired in 1882
Inv. E 112-3

This fine female head, which was acquired in Pisa at the end of the 19th century, would originally have been fitted to the body of a statue. The model is looking slightly towards the right, in a position that was widely used by Greek sculptors in order to give a work a certain asymmetry, which was seen as the generator of life. The massive face reflects a grave expression, suffused with gentleness. The hair, which undulates in three floating waves on either side of a parting in the middle, leaves the ears visible, and is gathered up in mid-nape into a broad plait, schematically rendered by a net covering the back of the head.

The work is similar to private portraits which, in the Roman period, developed within the tradition of imperial portraits that were of an honorary character, if executed during the lifetime of the subject, or else funerary. The introduction of realism into portraits was an innovation of the Romans by comparison with Greek sculpture. The Roman portrait, realist in the portrayal of faces, was also psychological: the treatment of the iris and pupil constituted a technical artifice which tended to suggest the intimate nature of the personage. Comparisons with the effigies of emperors and empresses, as well as the expression of faces and hair styles, make it possible to date private portraits fairly precisely. Stylistically, the fine face, which is a little static, and without any particular distinguishing feature, as well as the treatment of the hair, recall the sculpted portraits of the 3rd century A.D.
G.G.

Magna Græcia
c. 430 B.C.

Bell-shaped Krater
Red-figured ceramic
H. 0.31; Diam. 0.32
Gift of Renaud Icard, 1971
Inv. 1971-265

The bell shape characterises a certain type of wine bowl, a large open vase whose name, "krater", is taken from the Greek verb meaning "to mix"; it was in effect in such vessels that wine for banquets was mixed with water. This bowl is executed according to the "red-figure" technique, in which the silhouettes of figures and patterns are reserved in the glaze, leaving the red of the clay against a black glaze background; it is decorated on both sides with figurative scenes. On one side, three young men wearing *himations* are represented in a standing position; the two outer figures are holding staffs in their right hands, and are looking at the central figure, who has his arms hidden by his cloak and is looking at the figure on the left. In the main illustration, a woman, also draped in a *himation*, is flanked by two satyrs. A garland of laurel runs along the edge of the krater; the feet of the figures are resting on a frieze of meanders with crosses left in reserve. Judging from the style of this décor, it may be attributed to the "painter of Pisticci", who was presumably either an Athenian who had emigrated to Lucania or an inhabitant of Metapontum who had learned his art in Athens, and whose work, in any case, shows a perfect mastery of the techniques of décor and firing. In Magna Græcia, in effect, it was in the second half of the 5th century B.C. that local production began to compete with the Athenian vases that the Greeks living in southern Italy used for their tombs. The original centre of production was in the region of Metapontum and Lucania. The "painter of Pisticci", active around 430-420, was the first identifiable artist of this tradition; his vases resemble those of his Attic contemporaries. Certain elements, such as the slightly rigid drawing of the figures, the elongation of the bodies and the lack of originality in the motifs, are characteristic of the first period of Italic painted vases. Progressively, however, the artists began to show more independence and ambition in the choice and treatment of their subjects.
G.G.

Etruria
6th century B.C.

Three-headed Geryon
Bronze
H. 0.204; W. 0.085
Jacques-Amédée Lambert Bequest, 1850
Inv. L 1

The story of Geryon, the three-headed giant, is part of the cycle of the twelve labours of Heracles. Geryon was the son of Chrysaor and Callirrhoë, and his grandfathers were Poseidon and Oceanus. He lived on the island of Erythia, where he possessed a herd of cattle. Heracles received the order to steal the herd, and there was a struggle in which Geryon was killed. The figurine shown here is one of the very rare representations of this particular episode from Greek mythology. The triple image of the figure was obtained, simply, by the addition of a smaller head to each shoulder. The giant is represented in a frontal position, raising his right arm, which was probably brandishing a throwing weapon; his left arm, positioned below his chest, no doubt held a shield, which would explain its unfinished appearance. His garment, which is scarcely suggested due to the fact that it was probably dissimulated, consists of a clinging sleeveless tunic which stops at the top of the thighs while coming together in a group of folds at the level of the groin. The legs, from the thighs down to the ankles, are covered by leggings. The heads are wearing helmets of the Corinthian or Chalcidian type, whose crests have been broken off. This equipment was typical of the Greek hoplite. The rigidity of the pose, and the faces, with their almond-shaped eyes and fleshy lips, lend the piece some similarities to archaic works produced in the 6th century B.C.

G.G.

Etruria
5th century B.C.

Thymiaterion
Bronze
H. 0.565; W. of base: 0.265
Acquired in 1859
Inv. X 254-17

The *thymiaterion* was a perfume- or incense-burner, and was often found in Etruscan graves, where it lit up the sepulchral life of the dead person and spread a mysterious, volatile odour, which was the vehicle of the soul towards the hereafter. The aromatic substance was burned in a cupel placed on a shaft which, in this case, is constituted by a fine figurine of an athlete holding a column with mouldings, furnished with two discs. The *kouros*, who is presented frontally in his athletic nudity, in the Greek style, is carrying a dumb-bell in each hand; the position of his arms, which are slightly bent under the weight, is inverted in comparison to that of his legs, thus giving an impression of tension in the movement. In antiquity, the long jump was apparently practised without a run-up, the athletes carrying dumb-bells to improve their performances. The stand is made up of three sinuous legs ending in animals' feet and separated by shells.

This type of *thymiaterion* was produced in the workshops of Etruria, where, starting from the 5th century B.C., perfume-burners, candelabras, *ex votos*, etc. were frequently decorated with scenes of games and athletes.

G.G.

Roman Empire
First half of the 1st century
A.D.

Pyxis
Glass blown in a mould
H. 0.077; W. 0.063
Acquired in 1848
Inv. E 328-c

The blown glass technique, which appeared on the Syro-Palestinian coast in the 1st century B.C., was already widespread in the provinces of the Roman empire at the start of the Christian era; its low cost was conducive to the production of large numbers of vases and everyday objects. This glass pyxis was a recipient for cosmetics and unguents, but could also be used for toilet objects. It was made by the technique, which was common at the time, of blowing glass into a hollow mould; the decoration in relief thus obtained is similar to that of recipients in gold and chased silver. The cylindrical form, which is decorated with a chain of palmettes alternately pointing upwards and downwards, is closed by a conical cover decorated with godroons and a frieze of lotiform palmettes, also inverted, topped by a small knob. The fine deep blue colour was obtained by the addition of cobalt to the glass paste.

This pyxis, which was acquired in 1848 in a public sale, was reputed to have come from Syria; comparison with similar examples found in Syria and Italy suggests that it dates from the first half of the 1st century B.C. It perfectly illustrates the high quality that was rapidly attained by the Roman glass industry.

G.G.

Art Objects and Sculptures
Rooms 1 to 17

**Auvergne,
second half of the 12th century**

Virgin in Majesty
Polychrome hornbeam wood
and metal brackets
H. 0.71; W. 0.31; Depth 0.30
Acquired in 1934
Inv. B 1751

The Virgin, thus represented, seated frontally and holding the Child on her knees, is known as the Virgin in majesty, which is perhaps the most characteristic image in Romanesque art. The interpretation of the genre in Auvergne is illustrated admirably by the example shown here, which may have come from Saint Flour in the Cantal. This representation of the Virgin presents plastic qualities which set it apart among the few statues with which it may be compared. The rigidity of the composition, with its powerfully asserted frontality, is tempered by the position of the Child, who is placed slightly sideways on His mother's knees. The configuration of the work suggests that it is of a somewhat late origin, perhaps dating from the second half of the 12th century. The system of drapings with fine, close folds, almost calligraphic in appearance, demonstrates the impressive mastery of the sculptor, and constitutes one of the particularities of the "Auvergnate" style. The gilded metal covering, adorned with coloured cabochons, is remarkably well preserved, and adds to the interest of this exceptional piece. Like its counterparts, it was an object of profound veneration. It constituted a link between heaven and earth, and was probably placed quite high up on the altar, but was also carried around in processions.
C.B.

Spain,
Catalonia, c. 1170-1180

Three Prophets (?)
Limestone
H. 0.780; W. 0.620; Depth 0.135
Acquired in 1934
Inv. B 1754

This bas-relief belongs to a set which comes from the old cathedral of Vich (Catalonia), destroyed in 1781. Several fragments are still preserved in Vich, and two others are in the museum in Kansas City and in the Victoria and Albert Museum in London. The original destination of these sculptures is not known, but it may be conjectured that they were placed on the façade of the edifice on either side of a Christ in majesty. Unlike the other figures, who represent apostles with clearly-marked characters, the three in this relief retain their anonymity. They could be prophets, figures placed there in parallel with the apostles. The three men with their bearded faces, strongly incised, are walking in procession towards the right. They are dressed in long tunics, whose folds are treated in a fan-like way, and are linked up by phylacteries which they are unrolling in a composition that is at once supple and rhythmic.
C.B.

Berry,
1150-1175

Juggler
Limestone
H. 0.60; W. 0.33; Depth 0.11
Acquired in 1881
Inv. D 140

This fragment of an archivolt, found on a house in Bourges, undoubtedly came from the neighbouring church of Saint Pierre le Puellier, now destroyed, of which the museum of Bourges has a fragment of the tympanum. Juggling and dancing at the same time, the personage, wearing a short tunic and a small coat, has just thrown a ball with his left hand, and is preparing to catch it with his right. The figure, set in a thick border, manifests in a striking way the submission of sculpture to architecture which was frequent in the Romanesque period, and has resulted in this celebrated bas-relief often being used to illustrate the "law of the frame" defined by Henri Focillon, the great art historian, who was a curator at the Museum of Fine Arts from 1913 to 1924. The style suggests a comparison with Burgundian sculpture: the elegance and precision of the relief, the taste for movement and the highly ornamental aspect of the drapings are reminiscent, notably, of the sculpted décor of the basilica of Vézelay. The inscription on the border, where Armenian characters have been identified, plays a purely ornamental role, but also suggests the presence of oriental influences in France during the Middle Ages.

C.B.

59

Eastern Mediterranean (?),
second half of the 6th century

The Baptism of Christ
Ivory
H. 0.19; L. 0.12
Acquired in 1886
Inv. D 313

The entire upper part of this ivory piece, which belongs to the first period of Byzantine art, is taken up by Saint John the Baptist baptising Christ. Standing with one foot against a rock, the Precursor is placing his hand on the head of Christ, who is represented on a smaller scale, and with the features of a young man, naked and leaning slightly to one side, with a dove descending upon Him. This representation of Christ, which is similar to that of a pagan god, shows the influence of ancient models. Between the feet of the saint there is an allegory of the Jordan, recognisable by the overturned vase. The moon and the sun, also allegorised, frame the scene. This composition, which seems to be derived from one of the sculpted ivory plates on the throne of Maximian, the archbishop of Ravenna (Ravenna, Museo Archiepiscopale), was designed for the centre of a page in five parts, intended for the binding of a manuscript. Stylistically, the work may be compared to one of the rare sets of this type that are preserved in their entirety, namely the famous binding of Saint Lupicin, now held in the Bibliothèque Nationale in Paris.
C.B.

France, *c*. 870-880

*The Adoration, Sleep
and Flight of the Magi*
Ivory
H. 0.183; L. 0.105
Jacques-Amédée Lambert Bequest, 1850
Inv. L 403

This ivory piece, sculpted at the end of the reign
of Charles the Bald (died 877), represents three
episodes from the pilgrimage of the Magi to
Bethlehem as it is recounted in the Gospel of Saint
Matthew. In the upper section, the Magi, wearing
short tunics, offer their presents to the Child, who
is seated on His mother's knees. Mary is portrayed
in majesty on a throne of the Byzantine type. In the
middle section, an angel appears to the Magi during their sleep to dissuade
them from returning to Herod. Heeding this advice, the three decide to leave
the town by another way. Mounted on small horses, they are heading towards
the right, and the first of them has already half-disappeared under an arcade.
This plaque, which is of a great freshness of inspiration, would presumably
have been inserted in the gold mount of a binding plate. The stylised
acanthus-flower frame is a survival from the antique decorative repertoire.
C.B.

Limoges, c. 1175-1180

The Crucifixion
The Majesty of the Saviour
Champlevé copper, enamelled and gilded
H. 0.211; L. 0.135 each
Acquired in 1884
Inv. D 284 and D 283

These plaques, which were intended to grace the cover of a liturgical manuscript, are thought to be the two oldest matching plaques from Limoges to have survived to the present day. The artist used the champlevé technique, perfected around the last decades of the 12th century in the studios of the Limoges region, which consisted of introducing enamel into alveoli that had been hollowed out in the surface of a copper plaque. On the upper plaque are the Virgin and Saint John, on either side of the Calvary scene. The sun and the moon, personified, are placed in correspondence with them in the upper part, and represent the cosmic scope of the event. The second plaque represents Christ in majesty, appearing in a mandorla and seated on a rainbow between Alpha and Omega, surrounded by the symbols of the four evangelists. Around the periphery of these two plaques there is a frieze of cruciform rosettes. The palette includes no less than three different blues, along with six other colours. Left in reserve, the most expressive parts — hands, feet and faces — have been engraved and filled with a deep blue enamel. Delicate foliage spreads across the surface of the copper, framing the figured parts, which are the only ones to have been enamelled. This vermiculated background indicates the taste of the Romanesque artists for vegetal stylisation.

C.B.

North of France,
c. 1260-1270

Triptych
Painted ivory
H. 0.187; L. 0.205
Jacques-Amédée Lambert Bequest, 1850
Inv. L 422

The central part of this triptych, which dates from the end of the 13th century, represents Christ the judge seated on a throne, showing His stigmata, between two angels holding the instruments of the Passion. In the lower part, two angels with chandeliers frame a Virgin and Child. The style of this ivory piece, which is particularly refined, is characterised by the elongation of the figures and the fineness of the faces and the architectural frame, which is made up of delicate archings. This exceptional piece has been attributed to one of the first great workshops of the Gothic period to be active in the north of France — that of the Master of the Diptych of Soissons, named after a diptych which is now in the Victoria and Albert Museum, London. The triptych shown here presents the particularity of adding to the central panel two sheets of ivory covered with "flat paint". These volets, which are gold-painted, comprise two sections: on the left are the Annunciation, the Visitation and the Magi, and, on the right, the Nativity and the Presentation in the Temple. There is a relatively thick contour which defines the forms and brings out the drawing. On each of them there are three bands, imitating mounted precious stones, which recall that the most precious ivory pieces were often set off with jewels.
C.B.

Central France,
beginning of the 14th century

Head of a Prophet
Limestone
H. 0.44; L. 0.29; Depth 0.24
Acquired in 1934
Inv. B 1753

This head probably comes from the church of Saint Martin de Cogny, near Thaumiers in the Cher department, which was partly demolished during the Revolution. Its dimensions suggest that it belonged to a large statue which was situated, no doubt, at the portal of the building. The massive bonnet above the solemn face indicates a prophet. The monumentality of this head is reinforced by the mastery of the execution and the impressive control of volume. The smooth features of the figure, which are nonetheless expressed in a realistic modelling style, contrast with the unruly hair and beard, which are deeply incised. This masterpiece may have been sculpted at the start of the 14th century by an artist who was involved in the construction of the cathedral of Bourges.

C.B.

**Île-de-France,
middle of the 14th century**

Virgin and Child
Alabaster
H. 0.91; L. 0.35; Depth 0.22
(including plinth)
Jean Pollet Bequest, 1839
Inv. H 6

Free-standing sculpture was highly prized in the 14th century, and this remarkable example belongs to a type that was widespread around 1340. The Virgin, her weight shifted gracefully to one foot, is wearing a cloak draped sideways which covers her right arm and is held in place by her left hand. The Child is playing with the clasp of His mother's cloak, and is holding a bird in His left hand. This work, which is similar to a *Virgin and Child* in the abbey of Pont aux Dames, now in the Metropolitan Museum in New York, has been sculpted with a refinement that matches the material used, namely alabaster, and the effect is heightened by the gilding of the clothes and hair. A jewelled crown, now disappeared, no doubt added still further to this precious aspect. The suppleness of the drapings, the elegant play of the curves, the fineness of the details and the personable faces make this group one of the most seductive representatives of courtly art, such as it developed in the Île-de-France in the 14th century. The 16th-century plinth, which at one time held a statue of Saint Roch (as is indicated by an inscription), is a 19th century addition.
C.B.

Germany, Biberach (Swabia), c. 1520

The Last Judgement
Polychrome lime wood
H. 0.550; L. 0.172; Depth 0.110
Exchanged with the Chamber of
Commerce, Lyon, 1896
Inv. D 678

This relief, which was probably placed on the predella of a retable, presents an unusual iconography which combines the theme of the last judgement with a votive image relating to the plague. The central scene shows, below the bust of God the Father, a number of personages from every station in life, some already affected by the evil, others imploring divine mercy. The two kneeling figures in the foreground are doubtless the donors of this retable. On either side of the scene, Christ and the Virgin are interceding in favour of the plague victims, while the lateral parts illustrate the last judgement. On the left, Saint Peter welcomes the elect at the gates of Paradise, while on the right the damned are falling prey to the demons and flames of Hell.

This composition, which is rich in picturesque elements, is the work of a sculptor who was in all likelihood active in Swabia, in the south of Germany. The penchant for lifelike details and the attentive observation of the costumes that were in fashion in the years 1510-1520 add to the effect of the highly detailed, painstakingly carved work on the wood itself.
C.B.

**Southern Germany,
beginning of the 16th century**

Pietà
Polychrome lime wood
H. 0.75; L. 0.54; Depth 0.16
Joseph Gillet Bequest, 1923
Inv. E 581 d

The "pietà" grouping, with the Virgin lamenting over the body of her dead son, was one of the most venerated of devotional images at the end of the Middle Ages. The remarkable high relief shown here, which was done in southern Germany at the start of the 16th century, shows the ways in which this type of representation was modified in late Gothic sculpture under the influence of Dutch painting. The Virgin is represented half-kneeling, and the body of Christ, turned towards the faithful, is resting on the ground, supported by Mary's right leg. The originality of the group consists in the drapery held by the angels, against which the pyramidal group of Christ and His mother stands out. This motif is in effect habitually reserved for the figures of the "Crowning of the Virgin", or the "Virgin and Child", an iconographical particularity which, combined with the beauty of the faces, the almost serene pathos of the figure of Christ and the abundance of the drapings, confer on this work, a large part of whose original polychromy has been preserved, a place of choice in the museum's collection of German sculpture.
C.B.

**Bartolomeo Di Tomme,
called Pizino**
Active in Siena from 1375 to 1404

Chalice
c. 1390
Gilded and enamelled silver
H. 0.21; Diam. 0.14
Jacques-Amédée Lambert Bequest, 1850
Inv. L 689

This gold-plated silver chalice, which is a brilliant example of the mastery of the Italian jewellers towards the end of the 14th century, presents a chased décor, partly covered with translucent enamels. Its maker, designated by the inscription on the band above the foot, was Bartolomeo Di Tomme, better known by the name of Pizino, who seems, if one may trust the archives, to have been one of the leading jewellers in Siena during the second half of the 14th century. This chalice constitutes the sole example of the artist's work to have come down to us, though he is also known to have produced statues of apostles for the Capella di Piazza in Siena. The person for whom the object was made, as mentioned in the inscription and represented at the foot of the cross on one of the enamels, could be identifiable as a Dominican friar, a stained-glass artist who in 1397 was working on the windows of the cathedral of Siena.
C.B.

Italy, Tuscany,
middle of the 14th century

Angel and Virgin of the
Annunciation
Polychrome walnut wood
H. 1.75; L. 0.51; Depth 0.46
H. 1.71; L. 0.51; Depth 0.31
Acquired in 1884
Inv. D 234 and D 235

This Annunciation group, acquired in Florence at the end of the 19th century, is one of the most justly famous sculptures in the Museum of Fine Arts. The two figures, which are reputed to have come from the church of Santa Catarina in Siena, belong to the rich 14th century Sienese school of sculpture, which was represented by artists such as Mariano d'Agnolo Romanelli and Francesco di Valdambrino, to whom this group might well be attributable. The Virgin is distinguished by the sobriety and residually Gothic grace of the pose. The slight displacement of the weight onto one leg, in the manner of the French Virgins of the time, expresses the surprise of the young woman, who is dressed in a simple clinging dress which descends to her feet. In her left hand, which has been mutilated, she would no doubt have been holding a book. The angel, more richly attired, is advancing with deference and bowing in a harmonious curve. Set face to face, the two figures appear to be related to each other by the meeting of their eyes, yet separated by the opposition of their gestures. The polychromy, which unfortunately is in great part of recent origin, accentuates the animated quality of these life-size statues. The faces, which are of great simplicity, express with intensity the inner life of the personages.
C.B.

Mino da Fiesole
Papiano, 1429 - Florence, 1484

Saint John the Baptist
c. 1475-1478
Marble
H. 0.67; L. 0.57; Depth 0.28
(including plinth)
Acquired in 1888
Inv. D 382

This bust, which is one of the masterpieces in the museum's Italian collection, is a late work in the career of da Fiesole, a Florentine sculptor who was sensitive to the influence of Donatello, one of the main participants in the renewal of the art of the bust in Florence in the middle of the 15th century. The model's features, which are strongly individualised, express the determination of the Precursor, an adolescent who is practically heroicised in the antique style. The strong-willed chin, the hooked nose and the lines on the forehead are realistic details which, along with the deeply hollowed eyes, reinforce the lifelike character of the subject. The particularly virtuoso treatment of the hair, like that of the animal skin, held by two clasps with large cabochons, adds to the quality of this work, which might be compared to two other portraits of Saint John the Baptist sculpted by da Fiesole, now in the Musée Jacquemart André in Paris and in the Metropolitan Museum in New York.
C.B.

School of Desiderio da Settignano

Settignano, *c.* 1430 - Florence, 1464

Virgin and Child
c. 1450-1460
Grey stone
H. 0.37; L. 0.37; Depth 0.05
Acquired in 1895
Inv. D 612

This fragment of very high quality, though it may not be attributable to Desiderio himself, is nonetheless a remarkable example of the Florentine madonnas that were so popular in the quattrocento. Sculpted in a beautiful "pietra serena", the work is marked by the extreme sensitivity of its fabrication. It borrows from Donatello, who was Desiderio's master, the technique of the "stiacciato", a very low relief which brings sculpture close to the art of drawing. The harmonious combination of curves and folds confirms this graphic aspect, echoing the fineness of the Virgin's hands with their slender fingers holding the Child, who is huddled against her; He is treated with exquisite delicacy, and possesses the graceful character that has commonly been recognised in Desiderio's art.

C.B.

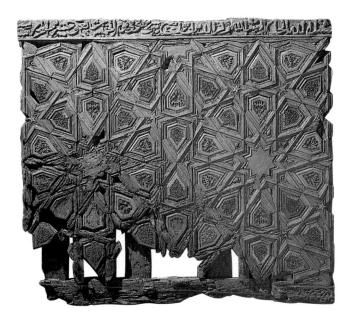

Syria, c. 1277

Element from a Cenotaph in
the name of Sultan Baybars I
Poplar, boxwood and jujube wood,
ivory and wood marquetry inlays
H. 1.18; L. 1.36
Acquired in 1887
Inv. D 351

In Muslim Egypt, wood was considered as a precious material, and was actively traded. Its scarcity explains the appearance, starting in the Fatimite period, of an original technique of assembly of small geometric elements, which provided a use for off-cuts while introducing effects of subtle polychromy.

This fragment comes from a cenotaph — a sepulchral monument constructed in the memory of a dead person but which does not contain the remains of the deceased — which a fine inscription in "naskhi" characters attributes to Sultan Baybars I, who died in 1277. This freed slave, who was the first great sovereign of the Mameluke era, led the army that took Saint Louis prisoner at the battle of Al Mansurah in 1260. This piece of panelling, which is extremely rare, is made up of sticks of poplar holding together polygons of boxwood and jujube wood, sculpted and inlaid with ivory, which radiate around two ten-branched stars, originally with marquetry inlays.

C.B.

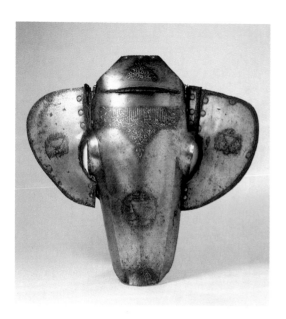

Syria, *c*. 1419

Armour for Horse's Head
Steel with gold leaf
H. 0.508; L. 0.555
Acquired in 1888
Inv. D 377-1

This chamfrain in wrought and forged steel, which is a remarkable example of the technical mastery of the metalworkers during the Mameluke period (1250-1517), has a fine gilded inscription in the middle of the frontal part, citing the owner of the horse for which it was intended, an emir of Damascus named Zain Muqbil al-Husami. The blazons of this dignitary, which comprise a document case, a writing case and a cup, sum up the successive offices he held during his career in the service of the sultan: master of the wardrobe, then second secretary, and finally grand secretary in 1419, the probable date of the commissioning of this armour in Damascus, which was an important centre of production of luxury goods. The frequent presence of heraldic motifs in Mameluke art expresses the high degree of hierarchisation of this society.
C.B.

Persia, end of 12th beginning of 13th century

Cup with Rider
Siliceous ceramic with slow-fire decor, lustrous and gilded over opaque glaze
H. 0.09; Diam. 0.22
Gift of Aziz Ezra, 1933
Inv. E 698

During the "golden age" which took place in Iran under the domination of the Seljuks (11th-13th centuries), several urban centres such as Rayy, and Kashan, and Gurgân were known for the extraordinary skill of their potters. The most sought-after ceramics, like this charming hemispherical cup, made use of two techniques of decoration, i.e. that of the slow fire (*haft rang*) and that of metallic lustre, which was developed by the Abbasid potters in the 8th century.

The bottom of the cup is adorned with a sumptuously dressed rider on a small lavender-blue horse, passing in front of a bush. Four medallions representing seated musicians complete this composition, which is surrounded by an elegant epigraphic band in the "Kufic" style. In terms of its subject, which is drawn from court life, and the highly graphic style of the motifs, the work is comparable to the art of the Turko-Iranian miniaturists of the same period.

C.B.

Persia, Fars province, 1347

Dish
Gold-and-silver inlaid brass
H. 0.115; Diam. 0.237
Raymond Tripier Bequest, 1917
Inv. E 542-22

This brass dish, which is a remarkable example of the heights of quality reached by the metal-workers of Persia under the Mongol domination (1215-1353), belongs to the highly uniform output of the Fars region, in the south of Persia.

On the spiral branches in the main section are six riders indulging in the leisures of the privileged class, namely single combat, hunting and polo. This decoration is related to a repertoire common to bronze-workers and painters of miniatures. The outlines of the personages, firmly stylised, are emphasised by a gold fillet, while the clothes and the horses' blankets are incrusted with small plaques of engraved silver, which have been partly conserved. The bottom of the recipient is engraved with concentric rows of fish arranged around a sun. A Persian inscription on the bottom of the base dates the work to 1347. This detail, and the beauty of the piece, make it a key reference for the study of works produced in Fars.
C.B.

Turkey, Iznik, c. 1555-1560

Dish with Fretworked Raised Border

Siliceous ceramic with a decor painted on white siliceous slip with a lead glaze
H. 0.075; Diam. 0.360
Exchanged with the Chamber of Commerce, Lyon, 1890
Inv. D 469

This large dish comes from Iznik, whose output developed to an extraordinary extent throughout the 16th century, facilitated by the authoritarian but enlightened patronage of Suliman the Magnificent (1520-1566). Its floral décor is painted with an exceptional sureness of touch, over a brilliant white slip. The fan of palm trees surrounded by two long strands of hyacinth form a sort of mandorla such as is also found on two dishes of comparable quality that are now in the Victoria and Albert Museum in London and the Metropolitan Museum in New York. As was often the case at the time, the raised fretworked border encloses a décor of waves and rocks borrowed directly from the ornamental Chinese repertoire. The range of colours, whose delicate harmonies combine deep blue, turquoise, lime-green, grey and very light maroon, made its appearance a short time before the famous tomato-red and coral which became a speciality of Iznik during the second half of the century.

C.B.

**Lyon, first quarter
of the 1st century A.D.**

Sesterce
Bronze
Diam. 0.034
Acquired in 1991
Inv. 1991-2

The sesterce was the Roman currency *par excellence*, unlike the gold "aureus" and the silver "denarius", which were used in general commercial transactions and to pay the army. The bronze sesterce was in widespread circulation in the provinces of the Roman empire, and its useful life often exceeded a decade, or even a century. On the front of this particular specimen, the fine profile of the emperor Augustus is flanked by his titulature, and this detail allows the minting of the coin to be dated to the period between 9 and 14 A.D. On the other side there is a representation of the *Altar of the Three Gauls*, the main monument of the confederal sanctuary built in Lyon at the end of the 1st century B.C. Besides its perfect state of preservation, this sesterce is of great historical interest, since this type of coin bears the only preserved image of this celebrated edifice, which was a symbol of Roman power in the capital of the Gauls, whence the dedication "To Rome and Augustus".
F.P.

**Lyon (?), first half
of the 12th century**

Seal of Humbert d'Autun
Bronze
H. 0.096; W. 0.054
Inv. S 83

In the Middle Ages, seals contributed to the affirmation of secular and ecclesiastical power. This particular seal is a perfect illustration of the sacerdotal type: the bishop is represented bareheaded, dressed in a long chasuble and a pallium; he is seated on a throne, holding a crozier in one hand and giving a blessing with the other. This stereotyped image is associated with an inscription, which also conforms to strict rules: the word "sigillum" ("seal") precedes the first name of the bishop, and that of the archbishopric for which he is responsible. According to this inscription, the seal belonged to Humbert de Bagé (or Beaugay, or Bargey), who was the bishop of Autun between 1140 and 1148, then archbishop of Lyon from 1148 to 1153. This piece, along with many other antiquities and coins, was discovered in the river Saône, at the Pont Tilsitt, in the first half of the 19th century.
F.P.

Pisanello
(Antonio Pisano, called)
Pisa, 1395 (?) - Rome, between
1450 and 1455

Medal of John VIII Palæologus
Bronze
Diam. 0.101
Inv. Med. Ital. 5

Unlike seals, whose criteria of composition depended on family membership alone, and thus permitted of no innovation, medals, which made their appearance in the Renaissance, gave a freer expression of the personalities and aspirations of the individuals for whom they were intended.

It was Pisanello, the celebrated painter of the quattrocento, who made this medal — the first of his career — with the effigy of the Byzantine Emperor John VIII Palæologus (1390-1448). On the front, the emperor is represented in profile, according to the ancient tradition of the Byzantine portrait, wearing a striking piece of headgear; an inscription in Greek, which was the official language of Constantinople, lists his titles and powers. On the other side, which is signed in the ancient manner in Greek and Latin, John is represented on horseback in a rocky landscape, meditating before a small tabernacle as one of his pages begins to move away. This medal was commissioned by Pope Eugenius IV, who was a patron of the arts, to please the Byzantines, who came to seek a reconciliation at the Council of Ferrara, in 1438-1439, which concluded the union of the two churches, then in Florence during the summer of 1439; it was struck in one of these two towns, and inaugurated the great tradition of the Renaissance medal.
F.P.

**Lyon, first half
of the 16th century**

Medal of Thomas Gadagne
Bronze
Diam. 0.103
Jacques-Amédée Lambert Bequest, 1850
Inv. Med. Ly. 15

Starting at the end of the 15th century, Lyon, due to its commercial importance and its geographical position, was among the first great European towns to show the Italian influence. Local historical circumstances (such as the visits, in 1493-1494 and 1499, of Anne of Brittany, on her return from Italy), as well as the existence of a corporation of goldsmiths who were acquainted with the new transalpine techniques, meant that medals were produced in Lyon before anywhere else in France. That of the banker Thomas Guadini I (Thomas Gadagne) was struck on the occasion of the construction, in 1523, of a chapel consecrated to St Thomas in the church of the "Florentine nation", Notre Dame de Comfort at the Jacobin convent in Lyon. Of this chapel, which was destroyed at the start of the 19th century, nothing remains, outside of some architectural fragments and Francesco Salviati's large retable, *The Incredulity of St Thomas*, which is now in the Louvre, Paris. Despite a persistent tradition, Gadagne does not figure among the personages in Salviati's work; and this rare, beautiful medal, which may be the work of Jacques Gauvin, a Lyon goldsmith of the Renaissance period, is the only known portrait of the great banker.
F.P.

France, 16th century

Armour for Horse's Head
Embossed and engraved iron
H. 0.48; L. 0.29; Depth 0.26
Acquired in 1810
Inv. H 165

The historicised decoration of this exceptional piece, which brings Roman antiquity back to life with vigour, illustrates the originality of French armourers starting from the beginning of the reign of Henry II. The model was provided, no doubt, by Étienne Delaune (c.1518-1583), who was a medallist, draughtsman and engraver; a collection of drawings which is now in Munich, and which includes comparable projects, confirms his community of style with the horse armour made for Henry II, now in the Louvre, which was characterised by the same use of low relief covering the totality of the available surfaces.

On the chamfrain, narrow ribbons structure the decoration while separating the different scenes of which it is made up. In the lower part, on either side of a broad palmette, are two powerfully muscled captives, among other trophies. The central medallion shows a furious assault involving horse-riders in antique costume. The battle scenes continue on the cantle and saddle-bow belonging to the trimming of the saddle, which is also in the museum. The gilding of these latter elements is well preserved, and gives an idea of the original brilliance of the work, which would have been worthy of a prestigious patron.
C.B.

Spain, Valencia or Manises, second half of the 15th century

Dish

Hot-kiln stanniferous faience
with metallic lustre
Diam. 0.434
Acquired in 1886
Inv. D 326

Lustre-glazed faience, which was introduced into Spain in the 12th century, reached its full development in the course of the 15th century in the region of Valencia, as this large dish, adorned with the a heraldic stag passant, remarkably demonstrates. Cobalt blue motifs, done free-hand on a fine, cream-coloured enamel, confined to the outline of the coat of arms and to the four floral motifs, structure the decoration as a whole. The fleshy columns which animate the surface in a continuous movement, like the interior of the blazon, were painted with metal oxides fixed during a second firing in a reducing atmosphere, that is, without oxygen being allowed to enter the oven. This lustre technique, which would seem to have been invented in Iraq in the 8th century, gave Spanish producers a long period of success with their European clientele, among whom this type of gilded faience remained popular up to the start of the 16th century. As is often the case, the back of this dish is entirely decorated in lustre, showing an eagle with outspread wings.
C.B.

Italy, Deruta, 1501

Pharmacy Jar
Hot-kiln stanniferous faience
H. 0.31; Diam. 0.21
Acquired in 1886
Inv. D 322

This *albarello*, a type of high cylindrical jar used in pharmacies, comes from a set, now dispersed, of which the British Museum, the Victoria and Albert Museum (London) and the Boymans - van Beuningen Museum (Rotterdam) possess other pieces. All are dated 1501, and feature the bust of a Moor with a headband, the emblem of an unidentified hospital. The yellow and orange background of this *albarello* is painted with blue curling foliage and a grotesque face with a bushy beard and large ears, on either side of a large label mentioning the pine kernels that the recipient would have contained. A crown of foliage and fruit forms a frame which is interrupted only by some mysterious monograms crowned with a cross with a double traverse. The series is thought to come from Deruta, one of the most important Italian centres of production of faience up to the middle of the 16th century.
C.B.

France, Limoges,
The Alleged Monvaerni
beginning of the 16th century

Plaque: *Pietà*
Enamel on copper
H. 0.17; L. 0.15
Jacques-Amédée Lambert Bequest, 1850
Inv. L 462

It was at the very start of the 16th century that painted enamels were first produced in Limoges by an anonymous master who continues to be known by an inscription that was deciphered from one of his works. This enameller's compositions, which were inspired by existing engravings, continued to bear the imprint of medieval traditions. The plaque shown here, which was the central part of a triptych, now dismembered, represents a Pietà. Seated in front of a Cross placed at the centre of the composition, Mary is holding Christ on her knees, with Saint John and Mary Magdalen on either side. The palette of colours, which features a great deal of dark blue and manganese violet, is completed by a remarkably preserved gilding, notably on Mary Magdalen's large white mantle with its broken folds. The faces, whose whiteness contrasts with Christ's body, are modelled with great care. The importance accorded to the vegetation is one of the marks of this artist.
C.B.

Italy, Castel Durante, 1530

Cup: *Giovanna Bella*

Hot-kiln stanniferous faience
with metallic lustre
Diam. 0.22
Acquired in 1884
Inv. D 236

This cup is one of the most successful examples of the *belle donne* series, which was a speciality of Castel Durante, in the duchy of Urbino, one of the main centres of Italian faience. The young woman in the bust is wearing a garment that matches her turban, which is adorned with bluish foliage. She stands out against a deep blue background in front of a banner on which is written the first name of the recipient of this majolica, which was probably presented to her on the occasion of her engagement. The charm of the piece comes from the contrast between the simplicity of the bearing and the ornamental profusion of the fabrics. On the back, the date and signature of the celebrated Maestro Giorgio Andreoli indicate that the metallic lustre with which it is partly covered was done in his workshop in Gubbio, near Pesaro, a centre of production of faience which was esteemed for its *rosso*, a lustre with reddish tones, of which it seems to have had a monopoly.
C.B.

Italy, Urbino, 1533

Plate: *Hercules and Cacus*
Hot-kiln stanniferous faience
Diam. 0.26
Jacques-Amédée Lambert Bequest, 1850
Inv. L 665

The decoration of this plate belongs to the historicised genre, which reached its apogee in Urbino in the period starting from 1530. Dated 1533, it was made by Francesco Xanto da Rovigo, one of the principal painters of this centre, who adapted an engraving by Gian Giacomo Caraglio. The scene, which takes place before a rocky landscape, represents Hercules, who can be identified by his animal skin, raining cudgel blows on Cacus, the son of Vulcan, who had attempted to steal his cows. The spectator on the right, taken from another engraving, demonstrates the dexterity with which Xanto assembled elements from different sources. This personage occupies the place of the coat of arms which figures on the plate, of which this is a subsequent version, in the Florentine Pucci family's set. The highly contrasted palette and the vigorous drawing show the artist at his best.
C.B.

France, 1535

Bust of a Woman in a Medallion

Limestone
H. 0.600; L. 0.565; Depth 0.245
Acquired as an exchange with the museum of Vienne, 1907
Inv. D 792

The highly salient bust motif, applied to a medallion background, was one of the most common elements of the architectural language of the French Renaissance. This female bust emerging from drapings, which comes from a house in Vienne (Isère department), was no doubt meant to be placed high up, which would explain the effect of perspective. The languid pose of the model, and her very fine features with half-open lips, constitute an image of disturbing beauty. The hair held in a costly fillet, along with the delightful little feathered hat and the large necklace describing a perfect curve on the largely exposed breast, add to the almost Ronsardian refinement of this portrait. Sculpted in fine light-toned limestone, this work, which may be attributable to one of the great manufactories of the Loire, represents one of the most accomplished examples of 16th century French sculpture.

C.B.

Pierre Reymond
Limoges, c. 1513 - 1585

Ewer basin: *Moses and Jethro*
Second half of the 16th century
Enamel painted on copper
Diam. 0.472
Acquired in 1810
Inv. H 459

Pierre Reymond was one of the most prolific enamellers of Limoges in the second half of the 16th century. The decoration around the raised central part of this basin, which held the pitcher in equilibrium, represents a Biblical episode drawn from the Book of Exodus: Moses, meting out justice in the desert after the departure from Egypt, receives advice from his father-in-law Jethro. The enameller, whose workshop made a speciality of objects in grisaille, produced a second version of this plate; it is now in the Hermitage, in Saint Petersburg. For these two pieces he adapted the vignettes that Bernard Salomon used to illustrate the *Quadrins historiques de la Bible*, which was published in Lyon in 1553. The gravity of the main scene, which is composed with assurance despite the large number of figures, contrasts with the playful and slightly irreverent character of the border, where, among other motifs, monk-hooded goat-foot sylvans prepare to make merry.
C.B.

Jean Naze
Second half of the 16th century

Planispheric Astrolabe
1553
Gilded brass
H. 0.240; L. 0.205; Depth 0.010
Acquired in 1966
Inv. 1966-1

The planispheric astrolabe, which was invented by the Greeks and introduced into the west by the Arabs during the Middle Ages, puts the celestial sphere and the surface of the earth into correspondence in the form of flat surfaces, so that the altitude of a celestial body above the horizon can be read off in relation to the cardinal points of the compass. This particular example is dated and signed by Jean Naze, the best-known Lyon clock maker of the 16th century. Born in the region of Beauvais, he served his apprenticeship in Creil around 1545, before moving to Lyon and setting up at the "Atlas" in Rue Grenette, where he made and sold watches and clocks up to his death in 1581. Clocks made by him are now in the Petit Palais in Paris, the Musée National de la Renaissance in Ecouen, and the museum of Kassel. This astrolabe is composed of a grooved brass plate, called the "mater", in which are set several verniers, which are themselves covered with an openwork part, called the "rete". The elegance of the piece, with its sinuous curves and the refinement of the engraving, makes it one of the oldest and finest surviving French mathematical instruments.
C.B.

**France, second half
of the 16th century**

Two-part Wardrobe
Walnut
H. 2.12; L. 1.55; Depth 0.59
Madame Ferrier Bequest, 1925
Inv. E 589

This monumental wardrobe, with its warm reddish patina, demonstrates the richness and renewal of French furniture starting from the reign of Henry II. The horizontals of the drawers and the entablature decorated with lions' muzzles, satyr masks and foliage are set off by the verticals of the caryatids, which alternate with the fruit-crowned atlantes who occupy the face of the wardrobe. The most original of the caryatids, applied on the sides of the upper part, present an abdomen of foliage, a feminine breast, and a lined, mustachioed face. The leaves of the upper part represent Diana and Vulcan placed in niches; above them are curved pediments, which are inverted in the lower part, where the divinities are replaced by heads covered with a folded cloth. This piece of furniture, with its typically mannerist decorative excesses, represents a point of equilibrium which was reached at that period between the cabinet-makers' taste for sculpture and their quasi-architectural ambitions.
C.B.

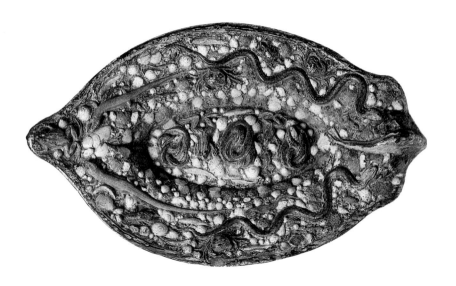

Bernard Palissy
Agenais, c. 1510 - Paris, 1590

Basin in the Shape of a Boat
Second half of the 16th century
Hot-kiln earthenware with lead
glaze
L. 0.755; W. 0.455; H. 0.138
Acquired in 1810
Inv. H 475

As the principal French ceramist of the Renaissance, Bernard Palissy remained faithful to the techniques of glazed pottery, which in the Saintonge of his childhood had been kept alive since the Middle Ages. The large basin seen here is an extremely rare authenticated example of this production; only one other, which is also to be found in the museum, is known of. This piece has recently been compared with a mould of identical dimensions which was found during a search of the studio in the Tuileries where Palissy worked. On a mossy background strewn with shells there are lizards, serpents, tortoises, frogs, crabs and fish, forming a curious mixture of terrestrial, marine and freshwater creatures, reflecting Palissy's interest in the natural sciences. His technique was characterised by the moulding of animal and vegetable forms from life — a procedure which in 1563 earned him the title of "Inventor of the King's Rustic Figulines". These were given a lead glaze coloured with metallic oxides, which covered the reliefs without dulling their outlines. This piece, which is exceptional for a number of reasons, also brings to mind the two grottoes in ceramic, now obliterated, which Palissy, who has become a virtual legend, made for the parks of the châteaux of Écouen and the Tuileries.
C.B.

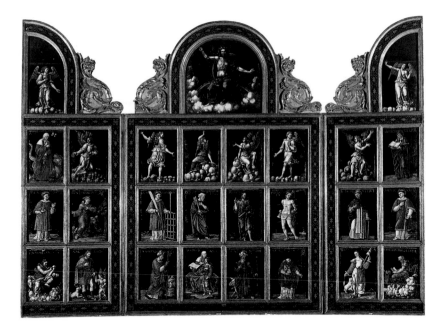

Limoges, c. 1600

Retable
Enamels painted on copper
H. 1.270; L. 1.775
Acquired in 1843
Inv. X 60-b

The twenty-seven elements of this triptych, which were mounted in their present frame at the start of the 19th century, derive from a retable, no doubt dismembered at the time of the Revolution, whose original location is unfortunately unknown. In all probability it originally had at least forty-eight parts, distributed among six levels, which would make it the largest that is known to us.

The enameller compares the theme of Christ's triumph in heaven with that of the Church on earth, achieved by her saints. The latter, who are identified by inscriptions in golden letters, are arranged under a row of angels walking on clouds, themselves dominated by a monumental Christ-judge. The artist who made these plates may have been Jean I Limousin (c. 1561 — before 1610); they are remarkable for the firmness of the drawing and the richness of the colours set against a black background of the kind which characterised the style of the enamellers of Limoges at the end of the 16th century.
C.B.

Nevers, second half of the 17th century

Dish: *The Drunkenness of Silenus*

Hot-kiln stanniferous faience
Diam. 0.533
Acquired in 1810
Inv. H 501

In the middle of the 17th century the workshops of Nevers, while remaining faithful to the "istoriato" genre, began to break away from the Italian influence. This large dish, whose palette of colours retains something of the majolicas introduced into Nevers by the Italians at the end of the 16th century, is indicative of an important development inspired by the French engraving style of the period. Nicolas Chapron, a disciple of Simon Vouet, was the actual author of this composition, which was adapted by a faience artist of refined talent. Old Silenus, seated in the shadow of a group of trees, is being offered a cup of wine by a satyr, while children play around them. On the broad border there are the same graceful putti, placed alternately in the cartouches and on the fine "undy" background, which is characteristic of the Nevers style.

C.B.

Rouen, second half of the 18th century

Hot-water Pot
Hot-kiln stanniferous faience
H. 0.222
Claudius Côte Bequest, 1961
Inv. 1961-191

This hot-water pot and its cover provide a fine example of the original style of the faience produced in Rouen in the 18th century. Its polychrome background has been executed with great sureness of touch. Limited at the start to five colours, polychromy made its appearance in Rouen at the end of the 17th century. The backgrounds, which are structured by bands derived from the famous lambrequin of Rouen, copied from the ornamentalists, are known by the term "à ferronneries" ("ironwork") because they recall the motifs of the wrought-iron balconies and banisters of the period. Ordered symmetrically on either side of a large motif above which is a small round baldaquin, curves and counter-curves decorated with thin drapings and small flowers stand out on a slightly blue-tinged enamel. Unlike the other colours, the red, based on ferruginous clay, is particularly difficult to fix by the "hot-kiln" technique, and is not used in large areas but in the form of dots or fine, parallel striations whose close spacing, seen from a distance, gives the impression of an unbroken surface.

C.B.

**Marseille, Manufactory of
the Veuve Perrin**
c. 1765-1775

Oblong Dish with Lobated Edge
Slow-fire stanniferous faience
L. 0.36; W. 0.23
Claudius Côte Bequest, 1961
Inv. 1961-228

The "slow fire" technique, as applied to faience, made its first appearance in France in the middle of the 18th century. This process, which fixes colours by successive firings at successively lower temperatures, made it possible to extend the chromatic range and, if necessary, retouch the décor. After Strasbourg, Marseille rapidly asserted its pre-eminence in this technique thanks to Pierrette Candelot (1709-1794), who was commonly known as La Veuve Perrin ("the widow Perrin") due to the fact that in 1748 she succeeded her husband at the head of his manufactory. This dish, which is signed with her monogram, belongs to a series which is particularly engaging in terms of its spontaneity of décor and the refinement of its colours, which are characteristic of this maker. The pink, which was absent from the "hot-kiln" palette due to the fact that it would not survive high-temperature firing, was called "purple powder of Cassius" at the time; it was obtained from chloride of gold. The central trophy is made up of fish, shells, fishing equipment, marine flora and floating draperies. The edge is decorated with other types of fish, as well as shellfish, and its outer edge is highlighted by a delicate raked pattern.
C.B.

Second half of the 18th century

Décor from the
Drawing-room
of *La Norenchal*
Tempera on canvas
Acquired in 1959
Inv. 1959-2

This piece comes from a country house, *La Norenchal* (now demolished), which was situated in Fontaines sur Saône, near Lyon. The house was owned by a notable citizen of Lyon, Pierre Monlong (1712-1789), who, after a distinguished career, retired there in 1762. Wishing to bring his new residence into harmony with the tastes of the time, he commissioned an artist to redecorate the main room of the ground floor, as well as an adjacent dining-room. This artist may have been Juste-Nathan Boucher (1736-1781), the son of the great Boucher; at any rate he was in Lyon at that time. This fine camaïeu decoration, which makes considerable use of *trompe-l'oeil* to enlarge and unify the space, bears the mark of the *rocaille* style, for example in the mock statues of "rustic amusements" (*Gardening, Hunting, Picking Flowers, Fishing, Harvest*) placed in picture windows which open onto a vaulted gallery diagonally traversed by a ray of light, to the right of the chimney-piece, overshadowed by a *Menacing Love* (after Carle van Loo). However, the strict orthogonality of the frames and the ornamental vocabulary, which is in the Greek style, make this drawing-room an early example of the neo-classical style, inspired by the discovery of the ruins of Pompeii and Herculaneum. C.B.

Macao, beginning of the 17th century

Embroidery: *The Death of Polydorus*
Cotton and silk threads, metallic threads and silk satin
H. 3.55; L. 4.75
Acquired in 1970
Inv. 1970-538

This embroidered work and its matching piece, also in the museum, come from a series of seven, of which some are in the Metropolitan Museum in New York. All of them represent episodes from the Trojan war. This one illustrates the sorrow of Hecuba, Priam's widow, on discovering the body of her son Polydorus washed up by the waves on the Thracian coast. Here the cartoon enlarges a vignette by Bernard Salomon from a famous Bible printed in Lyon in 1553, though the unusual treatment of the clouds and the sea, along with a certain awkwardness in the rendering of the drapings, reveal its non-European origin. However, the pieces of satin painted and stuck to the places where flesh is portrayed mark the taste of the person who commissioned it for the western style of modelling; the arms which figure on the border, with its exuberant floral décor, could be those of a governor of Macao in the 1620s. In any case, this curious product of a meeting between Western and Oriental traditions has been attributed to a studio in this city of southern China, which became a Portuguese enclave in 1557.

C.B.

Japan, Mino Oven, 17th century

Tea Bowl: *chawan*
Stoneware
H. 0.080; Diam. 0.136
Acquired in 1917
Inv. E 554-144 a

This tea bowl, which was produced in a workshop in Mino (Gifu prefecture), is of the type that was used in the tea ceremony (*chanoyu*), which became codified under the influence of Zen Buddhism during the 16th century. It is a typically Japanese object, and is distinguished from its Chinese and Korean antecedents by its rectangular profile and its shape, which was deliberately deformed before firing. Its décor displays an assured touch; it is of great simplicity, standing out against a fine creamy glaze. This bowl, along with 400 other ceramics, comes from the collection of the painter Raphaël Collin (Paris, 1850 - Brionne, 1916), which was judiciously acquired by the Museum of Fine Arts a year after his death. As an academic artist and a sought-after teacher, Collin welcomed into his studio young Japanese artists who had come to France to learn about modern Western painting. Thanks to the friendly relations that he established with his students, Collin put together an important collection of Far Eastern art, partly made up of Chinese and Korean ceramics, but which demonstrated above all the fascination exerted by Japanese stoneware on enlightened amateurs at the end of the 19th century. This type of art came to the attention of the West on the occasion of the World Fair of 1878, and had a profound influence on the Art Nouveau ceramists.
C.B.

Jean Carriès
Lyon, 1855 - Paris, 1894

The Warrior
Patinated plaster
H. 0.44; L. 0.61; Depth 0.36
Gift of Édouard Aynard, 1895
Inv. B 529

Jean Carriès was at one and the same time a ceramist of the first rank and one of the great symbolist sculptors of the end of the 19th century. He produced numerous portraits of his contemporaries — friends, celebrities and down-and-outs — as well as historical figures and pure creations. In this imaginary self-portrait, which is heavy with psychological implications, he represents himself clad in medieval armour. The strict frontality of the pose brings out the handsome face of the artist, which is striking in its meditative impassibility under an intricate conquistador's helmet. The expression, which is imprinted with a profound melancholy, seems to reflect the desolation of the battlefield, and to be, as it were, a premonition of Carriès' own decease: he died at the age of 39, while working on his masterpiece, a monumental *Parsifal's Gate* in enamelled ceramic. There are several known patinated plaster versions of this self-portrait, which was cast in bronze in 1884.
C.B.

Eugène Grasset
Lausanne, 1841 - Sceaux, 1917
Lucien Bégule
Lyon, 1848 - 1935

Stained glass: *St George
Slaying the Dragon*
1889
Glass and lead
H. 2.00; W. 0.94
Gift of Lucien Bégule, 1922
Inv. B 1280-a

At the end of the 19th century, Lucien Bégule was one of the principal glass-workers of Lyon. Between 1881 and 1911, his studio, which was eclectic in its output, participated in most of the major projects of construction and restoration of religious edifices in Lyon. Awarded a gold medal at the World Fair of 1889, this work, which had no set destination, was the first to result from Bégule's association with the painter and interior designer Eugène Grasset. The composition, which draws on medieval iconography, remains faithful to the great tradition of French stained glass, but the use — still parsimonious, in this particular case — of so-called "American" glass, which was characterised by irregularities of surface and colour, heralds the arrival of Art Nouveau glass-work. In the borders, an important place is given to plants, which are treated in an almost geometrical way; and it is here that Grasset's style comes out most strongly.
C.B.

Émile Gallé
Nancy, 1846 - 1904

Vase
c. 1898-1900
Two layers of glass, and applications
H. 0.165; W. 0.115; Depth 0.070
Claudius Côte Bequest, 1961
Inv. 1961-157

It was at the start of the 1890s that Émile Gallé began producing the most original of his works in glass. Under the influence of Japanese art, the décor of his vases, whose forms progressively diverged from those of traditional models, incorporated liberally interpreted elements drawn from flora and fauna. On this small vase, which is the finest in the museum's collection of Art Nouveau glass pieces, hazel catkins are associated with exotic magnolias. These motifs in very low relief, which were applied to the vase while it was hot, stand out against a background whose opacity is due to dust, naturally or artificially integrated into the glass paste; this was an invention of Gallé's, which he patented in 1898. His works, when as accomplished as in the present case, fall perfectly within the sphere of the symbolist taste for the refined, evocative object.

C.B.

Hector Guimard
Lyon, 1867 - New York, 1942

Madame Guimard's Desk
1909-1912
Pear-wood and gilded bronze
H. 1.114; L. 1.175; Depth 0.495
Gift of Adeline Oppenheim-
Guimard, 1948
Inv. 1951-37

This furniture comes from the bedroom of the wife of Hector Guimard, on the second floor of the house built by the celebrated architect at 122 avenue Mozart, Paris, between 1909 and 1912. This house was a veritable manifesto of his art, and contained not only living spaces but also his studio, as well as that of his American wife Adeline Oppenheim, who was herself a reputed artist. Guimard made this a brilliant demonstration of his desire to unify the totality of an interior décor. As well as the furniture itself, the architect designed the lights, carpets, wallpaper, curtains, metal-work, and even the tablecloths.

Borrowing from the vegetable world, and above all the flexibility of the naturally articulated stem, the décor is an integral part of the structuring of the different pieces of furniture. The backs of the chair, the armchair and the "duchesse brisée", with their overt gracefulness, are carved with elegant ribs. A continuous movement seems to permeate the small desk, to which a clever set of curves gives a singular fluidity of line. The bed and dressing-table make considerable use of a fine bird's-eye maple veneer, forming a particularly felicitous contrast with the pear-wood framework. This décor, which was donated to the museum by Madame Guimard when the contents of the house were broken up after the Second World War, is now one of the most important sets of furniture produced by the main French representative of Art Nouveau architecture.
C.B.

René Lalique
Ay (Marne), 1860 - Paris, 1945

Vase: *Whirlwinds*
1926
Moulded-pressed and enamelled glass
H. 0.203; Diam. 0.190
Gift of the artist, 1928
Inv. E 636-a

This vase, which was designed in the aftermath of the Exposition internationale des Arts décoratifs in 1925, is a remarkable example of the Art Déco style, of which René Lalique was one of the major representatives in the field of glass. In his highly diversified output, the vegetable model was often stylised in a spirit of clarity and geometry whose tempered modernism was never intrusive. Here the whorls in high relief, based on a bramble pattern, give the vase an almost sculptural dimension, which constitutes a veritable technical *tour de force*. The spectacular differences in thickness of the glass needed no less than three days of annealing at decreasing temperatures, not counting the additional firing of the enamel décor, which is rarely so strongly marked in Lalique's other pieces. Up to this time, the form had been obtained by the "moulded-pressed" process: the molten glass was placed in a mould, onto which a counter-mould was lowered with the aid of a piston in order to force the glass into the hollows. Where the different parts of the mould came together, Lalique deliberately allowed the joints to show. With this exceptional vase, which was one of the most expensive in the Lalique catalogue of the time, the artist proved that industrial production could approach craft-level quality.
C.B.

Maurice Marinot
Troyes, 1882 - 1960

Flask
1931
Glass
H. 0.107; L. 0.100
Gift of Florence Marinot, 1963
Inv. 1963-99

In 1919, after some years of producing enamelled glasswork, Maurice Marinot turned towards working directly on hot glass, and here he developed an exceptional technical mastery and an assured æsthetic sense. In 1927 he began to use a technique of "modelling very thick pieces made up of a single block, with heat and force", which resulted in individual works devoid of any utilitarian function. The "struggle between the breath that acts in the interior, and the pressure, the strain produced by the tools applied to the exterior, are two forces that come into play alternately", as he put it; this was a technique that generated simple, settled forms with rounded angles, like this remarkable rectangular flask, made in 1931. Its intercalary old-rose and moss-green décor was obtained by the use of metallic oxide powders, which the artist began using in 1922, and which gave the impression of extending his palette — recalling the fact that Marinot was also a Fauvist painter.
C.B.

Claudius Linossier
Lyon, 1893 - 1953

Ovoid Vase
1928
German silver with copper and
silver inlays
H. 0.263; Diam. 0.190
Acquired in 1928
Inv. E 644-a

This vase belongs to the period during which Linossier, a brazier who worked in Lyon, produced his finest pieces; these are of a very personal kind, and can be seen in terms of the return to favour of the metal-working arts around 1920. Linossier, who for a brief period was a student of Jean Dunand, in Paris, created numerous metallic vases whose simple, pure shapes bring out admirably the hot-inlaid motifs of the decoration, with their complex geometry. The shoulder of this vase is decorated with a skilful interweaving of two-toned silvery triangles, while on the belly silvery diamond shapes and large coppery triangles alternate in variable reddish and orange effects which are very characteristic of Linossier's work. The lower third, which is in fine plain black, is covered with German silver, an alloy of copper, zinc and nickel which Linossier added to his usual materials around 1922-1923. Thanks to a bequest of the artist, whose work is so engaging, the museum possesses a very rich collection of his brass pieces, as well as his sculptures and medals.
C.B.

Paintings and Sculptures
From 15th to 18th centuries
Rooms 1 to 14

Miguel Alcañiz

Active in Valencia from 1421 to 1442

Scenes from the Life
of Saint Michael
1421
Oil on wood
2.19 x 0.73
Gift of Francisque Aynard, 1917
Inv. B 1174-a and b

On 13 October 1421, a certain Mosén Bartolomé Terol commissioned from the painter Miguel Alcañiz a polyptych for the chapel in the church of Jérica in the Spanish province of Teruel. The contract insisted on the representation, in the central part, of Saint Michael, overshadowed by a Calvary and encircled by six episodes from the life of the saint. From this polyptych, since dismembered, nothing is currently known to exist other than these two lateral panels.

Thought to be of Italian origin at the time of their donation to the museum, and with many and varied attributions having been imputed to them, these two panels finally made it possible to reconstitute the personality, and a part of the work, of their creator, thanks to the contract in which his name is mentioned. He is known to have been active in Valencia, as well as in Barcelona and Majorca, and was one of the most active representatives of the International Gothic movement in Spain. This movement developed throughout Europe, between 1380 and 1450 approximately, in an immense burst of creativity. From England to Italy and Spain, from France to the Rhineland, the same decorative profusion manifested itself, driven by a common taste for elegance, brilliant colours and minute description, but without any realist ambitions.

Here refinement and a sense of expression define the artist's manner. The figures occupy all of the composition, leaving little space for landscapes, which stand out against a gilded background. The rocks lend their imaginary lines to the rigorous schematisation of the fissures and folds of the ground. The architectural features, which reflect the edifices of the period, control their perspectives well. As to the figures, they are remarkable in their poetry. Imagination is the key word, with real flashes of inspiration such as the group of angels repulsing the little demons, or the souls being tenderly welcomed and clothed on their escape from the fevers of hell.

V.D.

Master of Santa Clara de Palencia

Active in Castile at the end of the 15th century

The Death of the Virgin
The Crowning of the Virgin
Oil on wood
1.40 x 0.77
Acquired in 1862
Inv. A 2938 and A 2939

This panel and its matching piece constitute two parts of a large polyptych, now dismembered, which came from the convent of Santa Clara de Palencia, in old Castile. Only two other panels from the same work are known to have survived: a *Virgin of Mercy* and a *Mass of Saint Gregory*, both of which are now in Madrid, in the Museo Arqueologico Nacional. The anonymous painter is conveniently known by the name of the place of origin of the retable. These panels have been attributed to numerous painters, both French and Flemish, and indeed their style combines several influences. It now seems to be established that the artist was of Spanish origin and had acquired a sensitivity to Flemish art during a stay in Avignon. The name of Juan de Nalda, a Castilian painter who worked in Avignon in Jean Changenet's studio (which is known to have been in operation between 1485 and 1593) has often, plausibly, been suggested, though unfortunately the hypothesis lacks proof. The enigma could no doubt be resolved if it were possible to consult the contract which was drawn up between the painter and his patrons, who were perhaps princes. It seems, in effect, that Ferdinand II of Aragon and Isabella the Catholic are represented in the *Virgin of Mercy* panel.

The two panels show a very high quality of style: particularly notable are the clarity of composition (despite the large number of figures), the mastery of the perspectives, the sculptural utilisation of the light, and the majesty and gravity of the main figures, tempered by the poetic character of the middle ground and the picturesque quality of certain realist details.
V.D.

Master of the Pietà of Saint Germain des Prés
Active in Cologne before 1502
and in Paris around 1505

Christ Climbing the Hill of Calvary
c. 1503-1507
Oil on wood
1.037 x 0.962
Jean Pollet Bequest, 1839
Inv. H 651

Given the representation on the back of this work, in beige camaïeu, of *The Arrestation of Christ*, there is every chance that it is the left closing panel of a *pietà* retable (now in the Louvre, Paris), which was commissioned by Fr Guillaume Briçonnet for the abbey of Saint Germain des Prés some time between 1503 and 1507. The right-hand panel may be a *Resurrection* of which a photograph exists but whose present location is not known.

The scene, despite the violent gestures of some of the figures, gives an impression of calm, almost of immobility. The shafts of the halberds, and the accumulation of faces pressed against each other, intensify the dense, tightly-packed aspect of the composition, giving a good illustration of the abhorrence of vacuums that was typical of the period. The emphasis was placed on realism, which was dear to the heart of the declining Gothic age. The fineness of the painting, and the vivid colours, magnify the details, for example the grimacing, wrinkled faces, the grain in the wood of Christ's cross, the glossy coat of the trotting dog, or again the shells and grass along the road.
V.D.

Attributed to Claude Guinet
Active in Lyon in 1493 and 1507, died c. 1512

Saint Catherine of Alexandria
1507
Oil on wood
1.360 x 1.005
Acquired in 1897
Inv. B 564

This panel is in all likelihood the work of Claude Guinet, of whom virtually nothing is known other than that he was a painter of stained glass from Lyon, and whose known output, for the moment, amounts to no more than this retable, which adorned Saint Catherine's chapel in the collegiate church of Notre Dame de Beaujeu, and was probably a commission by Duke Jean II of Bourbon, who married Catherine d'Armagnac in 1484. It would in that case be the oldest "Lyonnais" painting in the museum's collections.

The style of the painting, which is deeply marked by Flemish culture, has often been compared to the art of Josse Lieferinxe from Hainaut (died 1508), who was a painter of the Provençal school. The elongated dimensions of the saint's body, her long, straight nose, the accentuation of the folds of her garment, and still more the sober, calm manner are all features which invite comparisons between Claude Guinet's style and that of Lieferinxe.

In the predella, the five canons who officiate in the chapel service frame the martyrdom scene; their names are inscribed in capital letters. The emblem of the confraternity is also reproduced on the robe of one of the canons.
V.D.

Gérard David
Oudewater, *c.* 1460 - Bruges, 1523

The Lineage of Saint Anne
c. 1500
Oil on wood
0.880 x 0.695
Acquired in 1896
Inv. B 540

This painting represents the descent of the Virgin, or, more exactly, the lineage of Saint Anne illustrated by a family tree, in the manner of the Jesse family, from whom, according to the prophecy of Isaiah in the Old Testament, Christ was descended. This subject was popular from the 13th century onwards on account of the *Golden Legend*, which mentioned the triple marriage of Saint Anne. The artist borrowed in part from the composition of a Flemish engraving dating from the end of the 15th century, to which he added two donors in prayer. This apocryphal treatment of the Virgin's family was much in vogue in Germany and Holland up to around 1530. The work, which dates from after the arrival of Gérard David in Bruges in 1483, and can in fact be situated around 1500, is sometimes attributed to his studio.

The golden background and the refinement of the interlacing that forms the foliage give this panel a certain similarity to the art of the illuminators from the end of the Gothic age. On the other hand, the costumes, the composition of the foliage and the modelling of the figures are motifs which derive from the Renaissance.
V.D.

Quentin Metsys
Louvain, *c.* 1465-1466
Antwerp, 1530

Virgin and Child
Surrounded by Angels
c. 1509
Oil on wood
0.545 x 0.375 (central panel)
Acquired in 1859
Inv. A 2908

The style of this small panel typifies the end of the Gothic era, and manifests the precursory signs of the Renaissance.

The architecture which can be seen behind the Virgin has often been compared to the chancel of the church of Saint Pierre in Louvain, in its original condition. On the other hand, the foreground, with its entablatures topped with columns in onyx, its capitals derived from the Corinthian style, and its semicircular arcades surrounded by putti, are features of an imagination which is strongly marked by the art of the Renaissance. All these architectural elements are subtly extrapolated into the small columns in false marble and the grisaille representing God the Father blessing the two angels who frame the principal scene.

The meditative attitude of the figures, the feeling of intimacy and the fineness of the execution recall the lessons of the greatest 15th century Flemish master, Jan van Eyck. The Virgin is characterised by an exquisite preciosity, and set off by the immaculate whiteness of her long dress with its golden embroidery, as well as the softness of her wavy hair, which is adorned by a diadem of pearls and rubies. The high forehead and long nose, the oval face terminating in a small pointed chin — these create an elegant physiognomy, as does the maternal hand with its slender fingers which emerge from a fur-lined sleeve.

V.D.

Joos van Cleve
Cleves?, *c.* 1480-1490
Antwerp, *c.* 1540-1541

Portrait of a Young Man
c. 1520
Oil on wood
0.600 x 0.457
Acquired in 1891
Inv. B 480

An old inscription in Indian ink on the back of this panel identifies the sitter as a member of the Florentine Gualterotti family, which is confirmed by the arms engraved on the ring on the forefinger of his left hand. The Gualterottis are mentioned in Antwerp from 1492 onwards as merchants and exporters of spices, and it is not surprising that a member of this important family should have wanted to have his portrait painted by one of the masters of the genre, around 1520. It is not necessary to advance the hypothesis that the painter made a journey to Italy. The painting is characteristic of the simple, "classical" version of the art of the bourgeois portrait such as it was practised in Antwerp at the start of the 16th century. The framing is quite broad, half-length, amplified by the background of blue, at once intense and bright, modulated from the bottom to the top by the treatment of the light. The attention of the viewer is initially caught by the eyes of the subject, which are forthright and yet almost absent, then moves to the hands, which are firm and strong-willed, holding a pair of gloves. The overall impression is one of calmness and monumentality.
V.D.

Lucas Cranach the Elder
Kronach, 1472 - Weimar, 1553

Portrait of a Noble Saxon Lady
1534
Oil on wood
0.530 x 0.375
Acquired in 1892
Inv. B 494

In 1504, Lucas Cranach the Elder became the official portrait painter at the court of Frederick III the Wise, Elector of Saxony, and immediately acquired great fame. The noble Saxon lady portrayed here has unfortunately not been identified, despite the letter W which appears in her *coiffure*, and the portrait of John Frederick of Saxony on the medal round her neck. The exercise is all the more difficult as Cranach's portraits frequently developed the same human type, and therefore tend to resemble one another. This is most certainly the portrait of a newlywed, in view of the numerous gold chains, which are incontestably marriage gifts.

The costume is the decorative element *par excellence*; it is opulent, even superabundant, and yet in no way spoils the interpretation of the face. Pearls and jewels vie in sophistication with the slits in the black-circled sleeves, allowing the white bodice to show through with the appearance of droplets. The tones chosen — exclusively white, black and orange — give this painting unity and incomparable force.
V.D.

Benvenuto di Giovanni
Siena, 1436 - 1518

*Saint John the Baptist
and Saint Michael*
Oil on wood
1.76 x 0.77
Jean-Baptiste Giraud Bequest, 1911
Inv. B 933

This is a panel from a polyptych which may have been done for a church in Siena, the birthplace of the artist. Benvenuto di Giovanni rapidly became one of the greatest masters active at the end of the 15th century. His painting reflects the Florentine Renaissance, but also seeks to resist it, or even to break free from it, and to adopt a certain spareness of line, which bears comparison with the art of Carlo Crivelli. This relative hardness is tempered by a great fineness of execution, a smoothness of touch and precious details, in particular in Saint Michael's garments, with a softening of the chromatic range, in which pink and golden tones dominate.

The painting brings together two essential figures of the Christian faith. John the Baptist is the last of the prophets, but also the first canonised martyr: he is the link between the Old and the New Testaments. Dressed in his short tunic, and holding the phylactery which bears the Latin inscription "Behold the Lamb of God", he is pointing his forefinger towards heaven, signifying his mission as a precursor. Saint Michael is one of the most celebrated of the archangels. He is represented here as a warrior, sword in hand, and with the dragon of the Apocalypse dead at his feet.
V.D.

Lorenzo Costa
Bologna?, c. 1460 - Mantua, 1535

The Nativity
c. 1490
Oil on wood
0.65 x 0.85
Acquired in 1892
Inv. B 495

Lorenzo Costa's *Nativity* is certainly one of the major works in the collection of 15th century Italian painting. It belongs to the first part of the artist's career, while he was still living in Bologna. It is the epitome of an illustration of private devotion. The scene, which is set in the stable of Bethlehem, with an imaginary view of the surrounding countryside, is that of the adoration of the Child: the Virgin and Saint Joseph are worshipping Jesus, who is lying on a bed woven out of branches and covered by a white cloth, in a prefiguration, respectively, of the crown of thorns which will feature in the Passion, and the shroud which will accompany the laying in the tomb.

Though classified as a member of the Ferrara school, Lorenzo Costa lived mainly in Bologna and Mantua. He was a disciple of the Ferrarese painter Ercole De'Roberti, whom he followed to the court of Giovanni Il Bentivoglio in Bologna; and in fact he became a citizen of that city in 1572. He later worked at Isabella d'Este's court in Mantua, where he succeeded Andrea Mantegna as the official painter to a sovereign who was known for her predilection for arts and letters. He participated, in particular, in the creation of her famous "studiolo".

V.D.

Perugino (Pietro di Cristoforo Vannucci)
Città della Pieve, c. 1448
Fontignano, 1523

The Heavenly Father in Glory
1495-1498
Oil on wood transferred on canvas
1.30 x 2.65
Loaned by Saint Gervais church,
Paris, 1952
Inv. 1952-6

The Ascension
1495-1498
Oil on wood transferred on canvas
3.25 x 2.65
Gift of Pope Pius VII, 1816
Inv. A 134

On 8 March 1495, the Benedictine fathers in San Pietro's basilica in Perugia commissioned from Perugino a large polyptych of fifteen elements, of which the Musée des Beaux-Arts in Lyon is today proud to possess the central part. The work in its entirety adorned the high altar, which was placed against the newly constructed rood screen between the nave and the chancel. The artist, who at this time was at the height of his fame, was the head of a large studio in Florence. He certainly returned for the occasion, with his assistants, to his native Umbria. But the quality of the execution suggests that Perugino carried out the major part of the work himself, and closely supervised the rest. The artist was required to execute the commission with great rapidity, that is, in two and a half years. The wager was almost won: Perugino took just four years, from 1494 to 1498, to bring the undertaking to completion. He also scrupulously respected the other points of the contract drawn up by the ecclesiastics: the use of fine gold and azure ultramarine blue, the precise iconographic details... A considerable sum, five hundred "large" gold ducats, was paid to him annually for four years. The polyptych was without doubt dismembered less than a century after it was finished, around 1591, and then moved around within the basilica itself at least twice. In 1797, the commissioner of the French government requisitioned the different parts of the work, except for some elements of the predella. They arrived in Paris on 27 July 1798, and starting from 8 November of that year were exhibited at the Museum Central des Arts. Between 1803 and 1811 they were distributed among different provincial museums, so that today there are fragments of the work in Lyon, Rouen and Nantes, as well as in Italy (in the Vatican museum and in the basilica of San Pietro in Perugia). In 1815, after Waterloo, the Holy See requested the restitution of the paintings: the panels which were still in the Louvre had to be handed over. But the authorities in Lyon, and notably the curator of the Palais Saint Pierre, François Artaud (1767-1838), had the idea of making approaches to the pope, and these proved successful. As a souvenir of the "tokens of devotion and attachment to his sacred person which had been given by the people of Lyon on every occasion when he had passed through that town", Pius VII agreed to make the people a gift of the *Ascension*. As to the lunette representing the *Heavenly Father in Glory*, in 1811 it was sent to the church of Saint Gervais-Saint Protais in Paris; in 1952, an exchange allowed the two central parts of the retable to be reunited.

On the explicit request of his patrons, Perugino represented "the image of God the Father all-powerful, surrounded by two angels holding the circle", in the upper part. This latter element constitutes one of the singularities of the painting: it symbolises the rainbow around the Heavenly Father, and was formerly materialised in the form of a wooden or stucco frame. This having been lost, and having in any case covered none of the original paint surface, it seemed preferable, at the time of the restoration of the retable in 1987, to allow the difference in tonality to remain visible. This painting summarises the art of the Umbrian master. The powerful, skilfully constructed silhouettes are arranged in a frieze, in slightly staggered rows, quite distinct from the landscape. The artist thus creates an elegant, classical rhythm, which was taken up all over Italy by the following generation; Raphael, his pupil, was profoundly marked by it.
V.D.

Bartolomeo Montagna
Orzinuovi, c. 1455 - Vicenza, 1523

Virgin and Child
Oil on wood
1.05 x 0.73
Raoul Duseigneur Bequest, 1916
Inv. B 1143

Three Musician-Angels
Oil on wood
0.47 x 0.70
Loaned by the Musée du Louvre,
1960
Inv. 1960-2

These two panels make up the central part of a polyptych which is now dismembered, and whose other panels are unknown. Nor has it been possible, for the moment, to establish their original provenance. In keeping with the usual tradition, the artist has taken up the iconography of the Virgin in majesty. The Child is holding an apple, the symbol of the temptation of Eve, and of sin. The throne is framed by two oranges, which represent fecundity, though also, no doubt, the blood of Christ. The three young musicians who are playing at the foot of the throne link the real and the spiritual worlds. Near the flutist on the right, and the little tambourinist, an unfolded white cartouche bears the signature of the painter: "Opus baertholomei (?) Montagna". It would appear that the top of the panel has been cut off, the upper part of the composition having in all likelihood terminated with a lamp. The dove representing the Holy Spirit, its wings spread out, watches over the scene.

Montagna, who came from the district of Brescia, does not seem to have travelled outside Venetia. The periods he spent in Vicenza and, especially, Venice, had a determining influence in the development of his art. Giovanni Bellini and Antonello Da Messina, passing through the city of the doges, were his major inspirations. He adopted the monumentality of their composition, the warmth of a vigorous light, the rigid beauty of the drapings, and the plasticity of the figures…
V.D.

Tintoretto (Jacopo Robusti)
Venice, 1518 - 1594

*Virgin and Child with Saint
Catherine, Saint Augustine,
Saint Mark and Saint John
the Baptist*
c. 1545-1546
Oil on canvas
1.93 x 3.14
Loaned by the State, 1805
Inv. A 122

Rare are the compositions in which Tintoretto shows
so much sobriety and equilibrium. This long frieze
draws its regular rhythm from the triangular masses of
the figures, which stand out against the great, stormy
sky. Placed in front of the white colonnade of a
temple, the Virgin takes on a particular monumentality,
which is further reinforced by the luminous halo that
surrounds her. Saint Catherine, with the palm and the
wheel of her martyrdom, occupies the centre of this
beautiful scenography, drawing in the eye. In the first
catalogue of the Museum of Fine Arts, which appeared
in 1808, it was noted that the head of Saint Catherine
differed from the rest of the composition. An x-ray examination which was carried
out recently revealed important modifications, and, notably, the underlying presence
of a "cornu", or ducal cap (which has the shape of a Phrygian bonnet) beneath the
face of the saint, who is wearing the traditional heavy mantle, with large buttons, of
the doges of Venice, feminised only by a light scarf. The figure who is seen in
adoration before the Virgin was thus initially a doge, who was succeeded by two
faces of Saint Catherine, as would seem to be shown by an attentive examination of
the different strata of paint. The face of the saint as it is now seen would appear to
be the result of a transformation carried out after Tintoretto's time. One seductive
hypothesis that has been formulated as an explanation for these changes is that the
election of the new doge, Francesco Donà, in 1545, may have given Tintoretto the
desire to obtain an official commission, taking advantage of the fact that Titian was
absent from Venice. Even before the election, Tintoretto may have made this *ex voto*
with a view to, as it were, putting forward his claim. Unfortunately, the work was
refused, and it must be assumed that the painter then transformed the portrait of the
doge into a figure of Saint Catherine, his patron saint.
V.D.

Tintoretto (Jacopo Robusti)
Venice, 1518 - 1594

Danae
c. 1570
Oil on canvas
1.42 x 1.82
Loaned by the State, 1811
Inv. A 91

According to the legend, Jupiter, the ruler of Olympia, changed himself into a shower of gold to seduce the beautiful Danae, who was kept prisoner by her father Acrisius, the king of Argos. The fruit of this union was Perseus, the celebrated conqueror of the Medusa.

Venetian painting was very fond of sumptuous, sensuous nudity. The theme was relatively infrequently used by Tintoretto, but Titian's Venuses are famous. Here the composition is dominated by the diagonal lines which trace the bodies of the two women, and the folds of the heavy brocades; it is characteristic of Tintoretto's procedures, as are the elongated dimensions and the plasticity of the figures. The puppy on the lower right, with its mischievous eye, attracts the attention; it is the invariable companion of the Danaes and Venuses of the Italian Renaissance.

This painting has belonged to a number of distinguished collections. Though the identity of the person who commissioned it is still, unfortunately, unknown, some think they can see in it a work that Tintoretto carried out in 1574 to celebrate a meeting between a famous courtesan, Veronica Franco, and King Henry III of France. It is known, in any case, that in 1624 the work was bought in Paris for the 1st Duke of Buckingham. It was handed down to the 2nd Duke, who in 1649 sold it in Antwerp to the Emperor Ferdinand III of Hapsburg, through the mediation of his brother, the Archduke Leopold Wilhelm, Regent of the Netherlands. The painting was exhibited in the castle of Prague at least up to 1718, when it was presumably transferred to the imperial gallery of the Belvedere in Vienna, where it was seized by the Napoleonic army in 1809.
V.D.

Veronese (Paolo Caliari)
Verona, 1528 - Venice, 1588

Bathsheba Bathing
c. 1575
Oil on canvas
1.91 x 2.24
Loaned by the State, 1811
Inv. A 63

The iconography of this masterly canvas poses an enigma. Though it is generally considered as a representation of Bathsheba bathing, some people have seen in it an illustration of the theme of Suzanne, though this would mean that one of the elders is missing. The story of Suzanne was much in vogue in Venice in the second half of the 16th century; Veronese painted it at least a dozen times, unlike Bathsheba, who was an extremely rare subject with him. It is possible that the solution to the enigma is to be found in the identity of the person who commissioned the work. In effect, the ewer and the casket placed close to the basin each bears a coat of arms. Veronese may have combined the two stories and adapted them to the requirements of his client, who was no doubt a member of the influential Badoer family of Venice. Moreover, the messenger's heavy cloak with its large golden buttons recall the traditional costume of the doges of Venice, and this might suggest that the Biblical scene masks a private representation, perhaps an allusion to a marriage between a Badoer and a member of another Venetian family, the Soranzos.

The painting dates from around 1575. It is known to have arrived in France very early on, in the middle of the 17th century, perhaps to become part of the collection of Gédéon Tallemant des Réaux, a cousin of the famous author of the *Historiettes*. It later became the property of Nicolas Fouquet, Louis XIV's Superintendent of the Finances, until the king seized his property in 1662.

As always with Veronese, colour is transformed into light, creating intense poetry. A taste for architectural décors and perspectives is manifest. The setting is monumental, with its imposing figures in the foreground, pushed to one side of the composition. It is skilfully combined with the gestures and glances which unite the figures in a subtle dialogue.

V.D.

Veronese (Paolo Caliari)
Verona, 1528 - Venice, 1588

Moses Saved from the Water
c. 1581
Oil on canvas
1.29 x 1.15
Loaned by the State, 1803
Inv. A 66

This work, which was painted towards the end of Veronese's life, sums up admirably the magnificence of his art. The composition unfolds in a crepuscular atmosphere where light plays the main role. The vividly coloured figures in the foreground contrast with the bluish background; there is a marked interest in the landscape. The scene is elegantly balanced: the pharaoh's daughter is matched by the soldier leaning on his spear, with Moses at the centre of two diagonals, above which is a luminous gap which attracts the eye.

The painter treated this theme a large number of times. This particular example is sometimes considered as a preparatory stage to the work in the Gemäldegalerie in Dresden. The Biblical episode serves as a pretext for the sumptuous description of a court scene incorporating a thousand opulent details: the silky effects of the fabrics, the sophisticated *coiffures*, the pearls and accessories… The dwarfs, and the black servant girl holding the puppy, contribute an exotic note of the kind that was highly appreciated at the time. V.D.

Francesco Bassano
(Francesco da Pontea)
Bassano, 1549 - Venice, 1592

Battle Scene (also known as
*Charles VIII Receiving the
Crown of Naples*)
c. 1585-1590
Oil on canvas
2.36 x 3.64
Loaned by the State, 1811
Inv. A 166

This great page of history has a matching piece, another *Battle Scene* (known as the *Siege of Naples by Charles VIII*). Francesco II Bassano, who was the most gifted of the four painter sons of the celebrated Jacopo Bassano, arrived in Venice around 1479. He participated in the decoration of the doge's Palace, before committing suicide at the age of 43. He was profoundly influenced by the art of his father, who, in his large studio, produced luxuriant, dense compositions which were most often Biblical, but were also pretexts for realist portrayals of everyday life. The titles traditionally given to the two canvases do not fit in well with historical truth. Charles VIII, King of France, took possession of Naples on 22 February 1495 without having to fight any difficult battles. Did the artist want to magnify the exploits of the king, or do the two works represent completely different historical episodes? They may have been done for Prince Eugene of Savoy; at any rate they arrived in France very early on. They were listed in the collection of President Nicolas Chevalier in the château of La Chaussée at the start of the 17th century, before being acquired by the 1st Duke of Buckingham in 1624. They were handed down to the 2nd Duke, then sold to the Emperor Ferdinand III of Hapsburg in 1649, and hung in the castle of Prague at least until 1737, when they were transferred to the imperial gallery of the Belvedere in Vienna. They were seized by the Napoleonic army in 1809.

In this work, Francesco Bassano has provided a successful description of an impressive commotion, with bodies milling around, canons and rifles spitting fire, flags and pikes rising up among the distant tumults… The range of browns and reds, enlivened by white and pink touches, accentuates the impression of frenzy. The description of this "contemporary battle", in modern costume, turns the work into a sort of journalistic document.
V.D.

Francesco Furini
Florence, 1603 - 1646

Saint John the Evangelist
c. 1635-1636
Oil on canvas
1.25 x 1.03
Acquired in 1987
Inv. 1987-3

Though he is known above all for mythological subjects with erotic connotations, Francesco Furini also did religious paintings, and particularly after 1633, when he took orders and became the prior of San Ansano in the Mugello parish in Florence. This particular work is one of the few examples of Furini's religious work known today. It was commissioned by the marquis Vitelli, the painter's benefactor and patron, around 1635-1636, and had a matching piece, *Saint Thomas*, whose current whereabouts are not known. This dazzling *Saint John* corresponds perfectly to the spirit of baroque Florentine painting in terms of its softness and sensuality. The model, who is of an ambiguous, not especially austere beauty, is also to be found in various of the painter's other compositions. The contrasted light makes the figure stand out from the background, and caresses his nonchalant arm. Precious details, such as the ink-well on the table and the rolled-up sleeve of the shirt, contribute an additional lustre. The scarlet of the drapings — a majestic piece of painting — entirely dominates the composition. This painting, which is one of the few by Furini that are to be found in French public collections, gives a clear idea of his talent, and of the vitality of the Florentine pictorial tradition after the Renaissance.
V.D.

Guido Reni
Bologna, 1575 - 1642

The Assumption
1637
Oil on canvas
2.42 x 1.61
Loaned by the State, 1805
Inv. A 123

In 1637 Cardinal Luigi Capponi, Archbishop of Ravenna, commissioned from Guido Reni an *Assumption* for the Lady chapel in the church of the Philippine order in Perugia. The artist was paid four hundred piastres for this canvas, which was integrated into a décor that gleamed with gold and stucco, still fresh, in a church whose construction was not yet wholly complete. Between the laying of the foundation stone in 1626 and the completion of the edifice in 1649, a new style of architecture, in conformity with the norms of the recent Council of Trent, had been introduced. On 21 February 1797, by a choice which signified the esteem in which the artist's work was then held, the commissar of the French army responsible for requisitioning works of art took just one painting, *The Assumption*, from the church. It was replaced by a copy; the original was taken to the Museum Central des Arts in the Louvre, before being sent to Lyon in 1805.

This image of the Virgin, which is of an ethereal suavity, corresponds to the development of devotion to the Virgin, such as the Council of Trent had advocated, and perfectly expresses the sensibility of the painter, who multiplied this type of representation. The work shown here can be situated between the 1627 Castelfranco *Assumption* and that of the Alte Pinakothek in Munich, dating from 1642.

Reni's inspiration oscillated mainly between Raphael and ancient sculpture. The present work, which belongs to the second part of his career, has certainly gained in lyricism by comparison with his first productions. The elongated dimensions, the undulating body and the little circling angels contribute to the illusion of movement and elevation. The tone of the composition goes from cold, silvery registers to the warm swirling of the swarms of putti.
V.D.

**Pietro da Cortona
(Pietro Berretini)**
Cortona, 1596 - Rome, 1669

*Caesar Restoring Cleopatra
to the Throne of Egypt*
c. 1637
Oil on canvas
2.55 x 2.66
Loaned by the State, 1811
Inv. A 53

This work was painted when the artist, at the height of his fame, was a prince of the celebrated Academy of Saint Luke, the painters' guild in Rome. It was commissioned by Louis II Phélypeaux de la Vrillière, Louis XIII's Secretary of State, to decorate the gallery of the mansion that he had had constructed by François Mansard in Paris between 1635 and 1637. Some years earlier, in 1631, he had acquired an important work by Guido Reni, the *Rape of Helen* (Paris, Louvre), which was the starting point for his collection. In order to form a consistent whole, this work served as a standard for nine other commissions in a similar format. To attain the greatest possible unity of style, la Vrillière made use mainly of contemporary Italian painters, among whom, besides Reni and Cortona, were Guercino, Carlo Maratta, Alessandro Turchi, as well as a Frenchman living in Rome, Nicolas Poussin. As to the subjects, apart from the *Rape of Helen*, they all had to do with Roman history.

The iconography of this painting remained mysterious for a long time, and many differing interpretations have been suggested. It is mentioned in a letter dating from 1679 as "Caesar giving back to Cleopatra the power that had been tyrannically usurped from her by her sister". After the death of Ptolemy XIII, Caesar did in effect restore Cleopatra to the throne of Egypt, on which are placed the sceptre and the crown. He drove out her young sister Arsinoe IV, who had been recognised as queen by the population of Alexandria.
V.D.

Guercino (Giovanni Francesco Barbieri)
Cento, 1591 - Bologna, 1666

The Circumcision
1646
Oil on canvas
4.15 x 2.65
Loaned by the State, 1811
Inv. A 65

The Museum of Fine Arts has the good fortune to possess a work which is among the most important of Guercino's classicising period, both in terms of dimensions, quality and fame. In the first part of his career the artist favoured a naturalist type of painting, with dense, vibrant accents and thick impasto, but when he reached maturity, and following a journey to Rome in the company of his Bolognese confreres Guido Reni and Domenichino, he began to temper his art.

The Circumcision represents a stage in this transformation. The composition has become more balanced and static, and multiplies the vertical lines (Saint Joseph's staff, the altar, candles and chair). Everything is centred on the Child, who stands out in a luminous halo above the shining altar-cloth. The colours remain vivid — for example the inimitable blue, which is a veritable hallmark of the artist — but the contrasts are attenuated, and half-tones make their appearance. The painter's touch has become finer; though certain figures, such as the priest, are still treated naturalistically, most of them, and notably the Virgin, have gained in classicism and idealisation.

The Counter-reformation, and in particular the Jesuits, brought the theme of the circumcision back into favour. This rite, which is a counterpart to Christian baptism, consecrates the Child under the name of Jesus for the first time. Furthermore, the blood that is spilled prefigures that of the scourging at the pillar and the Passion. The work was delivered in 1646 to the church of the convent of the Sisters of Jesus and Mary in Bologna, just four years after Guercino moved to the town, where he replaced the "first painter", Guido Reni, who had died. The painting was placed on the high altar of the church, above which was a lunette representing the *Heavenly Father* (now in the Pinacoteca Nazionale, Bologna).

V.D.

Bernardo Cavallino
Naples, 1616 - 1656

*Woman Playing
the Clavichord*
c. 1645-1650
Oil on canvas
0.79 x 0.64
Acquired in 1968
Inv. 1968-149

The works of Bernardo Cavallino, who was an individualistic, sensitive artist, are rare in French public collections. He was relatively isolated among the Neapolitan painters of his time, and his art can be compared, in terms of its subjects, to the sensibility of the poet or the writer. This gave him access to a large clientele of private collectors, for whom he produced precious works, in small formats, which often prefigured the grace and charm of 18th century painting. *Woman Playing the Clavichord* undoubtedly goes together with *The Singer* (Naples, Museo e Gallerie Nazionali di Capodimonte), where the subject, also turned towards the viewer, accompanies her singing by a gesture of her hands. Here, the young woman's long, fine fingers are delicately placed on the keyboard of the instrument (which was a precursor of the piano, and very popular in the 17th century). The oval of her face fits perfectly with the roundness of the canvas; there is seductiveness in the large, lingering eyes and sensual mouth. All is subtlety, particularly in the chromatic range, which uses a rare concordance of lilac and copper tones, the overall result being a work of great refinement.
V.D.

Guido Cagnacci
Sant'Arcangelo di Romagna, 1601
Vienna, 1663

Lucretia
c. 1657
Oil on canvas
0.87 x 0.66
Gift of Paul Chenavard, 1882
Inv. B 287

The painter signed this work "Guidus Cagnaccius / Inventor Faciebat", to mark his sentiment of legitimate pride. He no doubt painted it either during one of his journeys to Venice, around 1657, or else some years afterwards, during a stay in Vienna, while still under Venetian influence. The signature, which is so strongly emphasised, would seem to argue in favour of the latter hypothesis, given that in Austria, Cagnacci was just one foreign painter among others, and had to carve out a name for himself. Here, the artist makes a skilful synthesis between Guido Reni's idealism and Caravaggio's naturalism. He brings out wonderfully the delicate quality of the modelling, the transparency of the carnations, the palpitation of the blood under the skin. Lucretia, whose face and body are caressed — transfigured — by the light, is clearly defined against the dark background. The general tone is warm, soft and sensual. The blue of the ribbon falling onto the shoulder, the glitter of the ring, or again the dagger accentuated by a red line, provide touches of lively colours which come together in a refined way. Mixed feelings can be read on the face of the heroine: there is pleasure, but also sadness and pain.

Unlike the majority of the painters of the time, Cagnacci reduced the representation of this scene drawn from the history of Rome to the sole figure of Lucretia, the faithful wife of Tarquinius Collatinus. Having been outraged by Sextus Tarquinius, the son of Tarquinius Superbus, the king of Rome, and being unable to live with this dishonour, Lucretia committed suicide. Her tragic destiny was celebrated, successively, by Livy, Ovid and Boccaccio.

V.D.

Spain, end of 16th century

The Dormition of the Virgin
Polychrome wood
1.62 x 0.47
Acquired in 1889
Inv. D 415

This figure of a woman stretched out with her eyes closed, her hands joined on her breast, wearing a wimple, constitutes an impressive image of the dead Virgin. The effect is accentuated by the stunning realism of certain details, notably the rendering of the flesh, aided by the particularly well preserved polychromy.

The Virgin is represented here in "the sleep of the dead", during the moments preceding her Assumption. Initially, this reclining figure was no doubt surrounded by a group of personages representing the Apostles in prayer. Devotion to the Virgin's Dormition was very widespread in Spain. Such works are however rare in French public collections: this one has been attributed to the Burgos school.

V.D.

Antonio de Pereda
Valladolid, 1611 - Madrid, 1678

The Immaculate Conception
c. 1634
Oil on canvas
2.25 x 1.46
Loaned by the State, 1811
Inv. A 116

Known above all for his altar-pieces, painted for numerous convents and churches, Pereda also produced "bodegóns", or still lifes impregnated with a religious feeling. Pereda, who was the son of a painter, went to perfect his art in Madrid after the death of his father. He succeeded in getting himself introduced into the court of Philip III, where he found patrons, of whom the main one was Giovanni Battista Crescenzi, the Italian painter and architect. Crescenzi was a member of a leading Roman family, but, having been won over to the cause of Spain, he went to Madrid, where he became the superintendent of the royal buildings. He was even made a grandee of Spain, and Marquis de la Torre. He took active charge of the Buen Retiro palace, and put Pereda to work there. It is probable that the work illustrated here was done for his brother, a cardinal in Rome, who was an important collector. The work was first of all sent to the Eternal City; no doubt one of the Crescenzi family's numerous acquaintances was later responsible for its being brought to Turin, where in 1799 it was chosen by the French commissars to be brought to Paris. After being exhibited in the Louvre, where it was successively attributed to the Italian painters Guido Reni and Panfilo Nuvolone, it was sent to Lyon in 1811. This work is a good illustration of the painter's taste for sumptuousness and elegance. Warm, soft light envelops the Virgin, caresses the heads of the multitude of putti, and combines with the brilliant, precious colours, reflecting the influence of Venetian painting. A fine touch and precise drawing come together in virtuosity in the treatment of the Virgin's garments, with the meticulousness of the folds, and the rare, subtle chromatic nuances. The particular attention, characteristic of the Flemish tradition, which Pereda brings to the materials — fabrics and jewels, fruit and flowers — is very noticeable here.
V.D.

Francisco de Zurbarán
Fuente de Cantos, 1598
Madrid, 1664

Saint Francis
c. 1650-1660
Oil on canvas
2.09 x 1.10
Acquired in 1807
Inv. A 115

This astonishing work is the only painting by Zurbarán which is known to have been in France prior to the 19th century. Before the Revolution, it was in the convent of the "Colinettes", in the Balme de Saint Clair district of Lyon. François Artaud, the first curator of the Museum of Fine Arts, wrote of it that "the nuns put it away out of sight as a frightful object", and when a certain "M. Morand found it in the attic, his dog barked at it". No doubt put on sale by a junk dealer, it was bought by the painter and engraver Jean-Jacques de Boissieu, who sold it to the museum in 1807 under its former attribution to José de Ribera.

The convent of the Colinettes was founded by the marquis and marchioness de Coligny in 1665, and followed the rule of Saint Francis. The painting may have come from the Franciscan convent of the Descalzas Reales in Madrid, which had a very large collection of works of art, and was under the protection of the queen of Spain, Maria Anna, daughter of Ferdinand III of Austria; it may have been part of a donation made by the queen to the nuns of Lyon through her cousin and mother-in-law, Marie-Thérèse, the French queen.

The subject, which was introduced into Spain at the beginning of the 17th century by the Capuchins, who reformed the order of Saint Francis, seems to have been relatively rarely treated. There is an apocryphal tradition which reports that in 1449 Pope Nicholas V visited the crypt in Assisi where Saint Francis reposed, and discovered there, like Sixtus IV subsequently, the body of the saint, mummified and intact, upright in ecstasy. In any case the work possesses the power of this extraordinary vision. The saint appears in the darkness of the crypt, radiating a mystical fervour. The canvas plays exclusively on the effects of values, and intermixes tonalities of grey and brown: this sobriety only increases its expressive force.

V.D.

Nicolas Régnier
Maubeuge, 1591 - Venice, 1667

Young Woman at her Toilet
c. 1626
Oil on canvas
1.30 x 1.05
Acquired in 1975
Inv. 1976-7

The sense of this work, which dates from the artist's Venetian period, has intrigued the critics. Is it simply a young woman at her toilet, or a portrait of a courtesan, or again a Vanitas? The jewels strewn over the table, the bottle or perfume and the jar of unguent behind the mirror might suggest Mary Magdalen. The orange flowers — a symbol of virginity — which she is removing from her hair would seem to support this idea. The mirror, and the image it reflects, recall, for their part, the fragility of all things and the brevity of life.

The light, brilliant colours give the canvas an incomparable attractiveness. The ample, precious drapings, with their folds outlined by the light, create a climate of voluptuousness, which is reinforced by the disturbing beauty of the *décolleté* and the nape of the neck. The elegant head, in 3/4 rear profile, brings out the blondness of the hair, which perfectly matches the bodice. The blue ribbon which ties up the chignon sets off the wide skirt. The refinement of the details, and the fully-developed beauty of the model, make this painting more of a hymn to pleasure than an invitation to meditation and to withdrawal from the world.

V.D.

Simon Vouet
Paris, 1590 - 1649

Self-Portrait
1626-1627
Oil on canvas
0.45 x 0.36
Acquired in 1887
Inv. B 415

This self-portrait is generally taken to date from the period when the painter was still in Rome, a short time before his departure for Venice and France. At this date, he held the two highest honorary positions in the two countries: prince of the Academy of Saint Luke (the corporation of Roman painters), and official painter to the king of France. The artist is represented frontally, in realist fashion, without affectation or complacency: the head is round, the large forehead luminous, the eyes prominent, with slightly red eyelids, the nose long and a little flared, with quivering nostrils, the moustache and goatee beard pointed, the sensual mouth half-open. The tousled curly hair ends in a "cadenet", a sort of long lock that was very fashionable in Italy during those years. The painter has an air of simplicity, tinged with a certain melancholy in his eyes. The execution, which is brisk and full of energy, is well served by the brown camaïeu, which is brought out by the luminosity of the ruff.
V.D.

Simon Vouet
Paris, 1590 - 1649

The Crucifixion
c. 1636-1637
Oil on canvas
2.16 x 1.46
Gift of Cardinal Fesch, 1816
Inv. A 139

This work was painted for the high altar of the private chapel of the chancellor Pierre Séguier, one of the most important personages of the kingdom of France. He was an ardent patron of arts and letters, and entrusted the décor of the chapel in his Parisian house to Vouet and his collaborators. Including the central painting, this décor comprised twelve canvasses, situated above the wood panelling, which illustrated the life of Christ, and a painted frieze at the level of the cornice, representing *The Adoration of the Magi*, as well as a ceiling with *The Resurrection of Christ*. Christ crucified, with His luminous body turned towards the Virgin, is outlined here against a stormy sky. A deft interplay of gestures and looks connects up the different protagonists: Saint John's prayer, the Virgin's swoon, Mary Magdalen's emotion, the incomprehension of the two holy women... The vigorous forms, the ample draperies, the gestures of the hands with their slender fingers, impart to the scene a powerful lyricism, and the bright, acid colours add their delicacy to the subtlety of the composition.
V.D.

Jacques Stella
Lyon, 1596 - Paris, 1657

*Solomon Sacrificing
to the Idols*
c. 1650
Oil on canvas
0.98 x 1.42
Acquired in 1993
Inv. 1993-1

This painting is a matching piece to a *Solomon receiving the Queen of Sheba*, which was acquired by the museum in 1992. In 1693 these works were listed in the will of the painter's niece, Claudine Bouzonnet-Stella, and in the inventory of her collection. They figure at the head of these documents with high estimates, which signifies the importance that she accorded them. At her death in 1697, she left them to her second cousin Claude Périchon, a Lyon lawyer.

The two paintings illustrate episodes from the *Book of Kings* in the Old Testament. The first relates the visit of the queen of Sheba to the king of Israel, whose famed power and wisdom had come to her ears. Accompanied by her retinue, she brought gifts of gold, precious stones and spices. The second shows Solomon at the end of his life, when he turned away from the commandments of the Eternal and gave himself up more and more to the caprices of the foreign women in his harem, each of whom adored her own God. To please them, Solomon had sanctuaries constructed in honour of the idols Moloch and Astarte, and even made offerings to them.

Here Stella apparently wanted to emulate his friend Nicolas Poussin's masterpiece *The Judgement of Solomon* (Paris, Louvre), painted in 1649. These two paintings demonstrate his ability to create large compositions featuring historical subjects with many figures. The two scenes relate to each other in perfect classical balance. In a majestic interior décor with rich marble paving, lit by the morning light, Solomon, in the wisdom of the beginning of his reign, is set against his other self, making night sacrifice to the idols in the madness of his old age. And then there is the throne of Israel, matched by that of the divinity with the bull's head, while static, solemn figures correspond to frenzied dances.
V.D.

Jacques Stella
Lyon, 1596 - Paris, 1657

Self-Portrait
c. 1650
Oil on canvas
0.83 x 0.67
Acquired in 1856
Inv. A 2886

This portrait, with its mysterious expression, has long intrigued the critics, not on account of the identity of the sitter, which was confirmed by an engraving and by other portraits, but by its autographic character. Numerous names (in particular those of Flemish and Dutch painters) were suggested before the work was finally attributed to Stella. It is generally taken to date from his Parisian period. The painter, who was an epistolary friend of Nicolas Poussin, represents himself half-length, holding a rolled-up drawing, with a grave, weary air (a sign of his precarious state of health), in a description without concession: the large forehead is high and rounded, the eyes piercing and attentive, the nose broad and flat, the cheeks hollow, the lips thick under a flourishing moustache, the hair flat... The rapid brush-strokes bring out the subtle play of black tones in the garments.
V.D.

Jacques Blanchard
Paris, 1600 - 1638

Danae
c. 1631-1633
Oil on canvas
0.93 x 1.30
Acquired in 1990
Inv. 1990-71

Throughout his all-too-brief career, Jacques Blanchard was a fervent painter of feminine beauty; this *Danae*, in its undissimulated sensuality and eroticism, is a characteristic demonstration of the fact. There exists another version, in the Pushkin museum in Moscow; it is a more highly "dressed" version, as well as being slightly different in the organisation of the drapings, and was certainly painted for an amateur. The two paintings were evidently produced at the beginning of Blanchard's stay in Paris, soon after his return from Venice, where he had spent two years.

The affiliation with Venetian painting — in particular the influence of Titian — is very noticeable here. The brilliant execution, added to the decorative effect of the red drapings with their golden edgings, and the shimmering colours, are what give the painting its sumptuous character. The dense composition with its energetic lines is reinforced by the vigorous touch, the powerful modelling and the strong luminous contrasts. The female servant, seen from behind, imposes her sombre mass on the foreground and gives the scene its profundity, while setting off Danae's brilliant carnation.
V.D.

Philippe de Champaigne
Brussels, 1602 - Paris, 1674

The Adoration of the Shepherds
1628
Oil on canvas
3.97 x 2.47
Loaned by the State, 1805
Inv. A 52

This painting was commissioned by Marie de Médicis in 1628 for the nave of the church in the convent of the Faubourg Saint Jacques in Paris. The painter, who was the official painter to the queen of France, was later asked to produce four other compositions. Some were also, in part, the fruit of the liberality of pious donors, like the one presented here, which shows the arms of a noble family in the lower left corner. It was seized during the Revolution, and sent to the Museum Central des Arts in Paris, before coming to Lyon in 1805.

Three episodes from the birth of Christ are brought together here in the same work: the nativity in the foreground, the annunciation to the shepherds on the right in the background, and the adoration of the shepherds hurrying to bow down before the Child. The little angels flying around or playing with a phylactery represent the celestial militia.

This work signifies a turning point in the painter's career, where Flemish, Italian and French influences are combined. In the chiaroscuro composition, the brilliance of the white linen draws the eye towards the Child. The realistic treatment of the shepherds constitutes a real gallery of highly individualised portraits. The lamb that has been brought as a gift, and the dog, sitting quietly, are other characteristics of the Flemish naturalism in which the artist was still immersed.

V.D.

Charles Le Brun
Paris, 1619 - 1690

The Resurrection of Christ
1674-1676
Oil on canvas
4.80 x 2.65
Loaned by the State, 1811
Inv. A 203

This *Resurrection of Christ* has all the characteristics of a royal *ex voto*, though indeed the custom fell into disuse during the second half of the 17th century. Louis XIV borrowed the considerable sum of 50,000 livres from the powerful mercers' corporation to finance his war against the Spanish in Franche-Comté. After his victory, the king accompanied the reimbursement of his debt with a sum of money to pay for the decoration of the mercers' chapel in the church of Saint Sepulchre in Paris, as well as for prayers to be said for him. Through the mediation of Colbert, the mercers asked Charles Le Brun, who at the time was working at Versailles, to do a painting for the high altar of the chancel. The commission was finalised in 1674, and the painting installed on 20 August 1676.

In this allegory religion and contemporary history come together. Saint Louis, king of France and patron of the mercers' corporation, presents Louis XIV, wearing his royal cloak and the arms of the warlord, to the resurrected Christ. Louis XIV offers God his sceptre and helmet. Colbert's left hand designates the riches his government has procured; these are placed in a vase with handles in the form of snakes, which figure in his coat of arms. In the lower left corner is the shield of the mercers' corporation, with their motto above it. The hierarchical arrangement of the figures emphasises the divine essence of the monarchy of Louis XIV, who is shown young and victorious, in the image of Christ exalted in light. The fear on the faces of the defeated soldiers speaks eloquently of the artist's interest in the representation of emotions. A baroque streak runs through this great coloured tableau, though it is tempered by the classicism of the Raphaelesque human types, and the frontal presentation of the faces.

V.D.

Philippe de Champaigne
Brussels, 1602 - Paris, 1674

*The Invention of the Relics
of Saint Gervais and
Saint Protais*
1657-1660
Oil on canvas
3.60 x 6.81
Loaned by the State, 1811
Inv. A 103

In 1652, six large cartoons for tapestries recounting the history of the patron saints of the church of Saint Gervais-Saint Protais in Paris were commissioned by the wardens of the parish from Eustache Le Sueur, who died in 1655 after executing only the first two: *Saint Gervais and Saint Protais, Brought before Astasius, Refuse to Sacrifice to Jupiter* (Paris, Louvre) and *The Martyrdom of Saint Protais* (Museum of Fine Arts), which was completed by his brother-in-law Thomas Goussé. *The Martyrdom of Saint Protais* (Arras, Musée des Beaux Arts) was entrusted to Sébastien Bourdon, who presumably failed to give satisfaction since Philippe de Champaigne was called on for the last three compositions. As regards the painting which is now in Lyon, the artist signed a contract on 2 February 1657; the work was completed on 24 March 1660, at which time he received payment of 1,100 livres. The dimensions of the cartoons were determined by the spacing between the pillars of the nave of the church, where the full set went on permanent exhibition. The tapestries, whose delivery began in 1661, were shown on feast days in the chancel and the transept.

Saint Gervais and Saint Protais, who were sons of Saints Vital and Valerie, were benefactors of the poor. They were arrested by order of Nero: one was flagellated, the other decapitated. In the year 386, Saint Ambrose, the bishop of Milan, exhumed the bodies, which were found to be miraculously preserved, and transferred them to the basilica of Milan which later took his name.

The choice of the iconographical programme, and its expression in a realism without concession, derived from the revival of the worship of these saints, which had begun after the Council of Trent. The two-tier composition, with the numerous figures milling round the rostrum to get a better look at the scene, accentuates the atmosphere of drama.

V.D.

Jean-Baptiste Jouvenet
Rouen, 1644 - Paris, 1717

The Feast in the House of Simon
1706
Oil on canvas
3.93 x 6.63
Loaned by the State, 1811
Inv. A 205

Along with *The Money-Changers Driven out of the Temple* (which is exhibited in the same room), *The Resurrection of Lazarus* and *The Miracle of the Fishes* (Paris, Louvre), this huge canvas adorned the nave of the Benedictine priory of Saint Martin des Champs in Paris. The first three paintings, when they were shown in the Paris Salon of 1704, had to be exhibited in the courtyard of the Louvre on account of their size. The full series, almost completed, was presented to Louis XIV at the Trianon palace in July 1705. The king, much impressed, ordered a transcription into tapestry form, and this was started in 1711. The four paintings arrived in the Parisian church only at the end of 1706, due to the fact that the Benedictine monks were short of funds and could not pay the painter.

Jouvenet treats this episode from the Gospel according to Saint Luke as an epic tale, allowing the spectator to participate in the scene. Jesus, who is a guest at a feast in the house of Simon the Pharisee, sees a woman with her hair undone kneel in front of him and anoint his feet with perfume. When Simon reproaches Jesus for allowing himself to be touched by a courtesan, Jesus replies that he has forgiven her her numerous sins because she has shown much love. He addes: "He to whom little is forgiven, the same loveth little".

The frieze composition, with its skilful use of diagonals played off against one other, creates an imposing overall effect. A multitude of figures with expressive faces and gestures, and vigorous, massive anatomies, appear to rush round in all directions, but this does not affect the legibility of the scene. In this composition, where even the painter and his family are bustling round the rostrum on the right, calling on the spectator as a witness, only Mary Magdalen seems static. The colours, which are simple and brilliant, attest to the indisputable triumph, in French painting, of the "Rubenists" over the "Poussinists", who gave primacy to drawing.

V.D.

Peter-Paul Rubens
Siegen, 1577 - Antwerp, 1640

Saint Dominic and Saint Francis of Assisi Protecting the World from the Anger of Christ
c. 1618-1620
Oil on canvas
5.65 x 3.65
Loaned by the State, 1811
Inv. A 194

This painting was hung above the high altar of the Dominican church of Saint Paul in Antwerp. It was no doubt commissioned during the period of reconstruction and redecoration of the church by Michiel Ophovius, the prior of the Dominican monastery. And this fervent defender of the Counter-reformation was presumably responsible for the design of the iconographical programme. According to a medieval legend, Saint Dominic had a vision of Christ allowing his anger to explode against humanity, which had given itself up to its three principal sins: pride, covetousness and lust. Here Saint Dominic in his black cloak (whose features are very probably those of Michiel Ophovius) and Saint Francis in his brown robe succeed in leading the world back to the path of virtue. Both have taken vows of obedience, poverty and chastity, and they alone can protect the world from the three bolts of lightning which Christ is preparing to hurl, in spite of the Virgin's attempts to hold Him back. In the upper part of this tumultuous scene, Christ, surrounded by clouds, is transformed into an Olympian Zeus brandishing the lightning bolts. Below, the areopagus of saints forms a colourful, animated counterpoise.
V.D.

Peter Paul Rubens
Siegen, 1577 - Antwerp, 1640

The Adoration of the Magi
c. 1617-1618
Oil on canvas
2.51 x 3.28
Loaned by the State, 1805
Inv. A 118

The Adoration of the Magi was one of Rubens's favourite themes; he treated it at least ten times. The painting shown here was done in 1621. The identity of the person who commissioned it is unfortunately unknown. The horizontal format makes it improbable that it was a religious commission, intended for the décoration of an altar. In the 18th century it appeared in Munich, in the prestigious collection of the Electors of Bavaria, where it may in fact have arrived even earlier.

Organised in a large baroque diagonal, the sumptuous cortege leans over towards the Child. The typically Flemish magnificence of the rendering of the fabrics contrasts with the simplicity of the Holy Family group. And in the same way, the solemnity of the Magi contrasts with the fragility of Jesus, whose hand seems tiny on the imposing bald head. The saffron-yellow robe worn by the Ethiopian king, with his almost insolent frontality, matches that of the king, who is seen kneeling; and the small fragment of sky matches the colour of the Virgin's robe.

V.D.

Jacob Jordaens
Antwerp, 1593 - 1678

Mercury and Argus
c. 1620
Oil on canvas
2.02 x 2.41
Acquired in 1843
Inv. H 679

Jordaens treats this episode from Ovid's *Metamorphoses* in a way that is at once spectacular and realistic. The scene is approaching its dénouement: the god Mercury, disguised as a shepherd, is getting ready to save Io, who has been transformed into a white cow by Jupiter, the ruler of Olympia, in order to safeguard her from the jealousy of Juno, his queen. Mercury is preparing to cut off the head of Io's hundred-eyed guardian, the giant Argus, whom he has put to sleep with his flute, then with a monotonous story. Jordaens takes some liberties with Ovid's text: Mercury is wearing a simple shepherd's hat, and not his winged petasus, and Argus is no more than a dozing old man, not a hybrid being with a hundred eyes.

The painting makes skilful use of a point of view which is at once very close-up and also seen as if from below, which reinforces the dramatic effect for the spectator. Powerful foreshortenings also amplify the very strong presence of the animals and the vegetation, and bring out the crude naturalism of certain details, such as the dirty feet of the two protagonists, and Argus's old, wrinkled body. The cows and the big immobile dog illustrate Jordaens's talent as an animal painter. And in fact he used notations taken from life, as is shown by the oil sketch for *Five Studies of Cows* (Lille, Musée des Beaux-Arts), in which there are two representations, though back to front, of the brown cow seen on the left in the painting shown here. This method also held good for the portraits; for example, Argus's hirsute head, which also appears in other compositions, undoubtedly derives from one of the heads of old men, or "apostles", which the young Van Dyck and Jordaens turned out repeatedly in Rubens's studio.
V.D.

Frans Snyders
Antwerp, 1579 - 1657

*Kitchen Table with Game
and Vegetables*
c. 1620-1630
Oil on canvas
2.72 x 3.37
Loaned by the State, 1811
Inv. A 117

Snyders was the uncontested specialist of large baroque still lifes in Flanders in the first half of the 17th century. The motif of the kitchen table on which there is a pile of game forms a part of the great tradition of stalls in the market and butcher's shops, inaugurated in the previous century by Pieter Aertsen and later propagated by Joachim Beuckelaer. The dead swan's light-coloured form constitutes the central point of the composition, around which everything else is organised. The picturesque detail of the cat and its little ones taking advantage of the fact that the dog is asleep to improve their usual menu introduces a narrative element into this inventory of the hunting arts.

On the right, in the place of the central part of the brick wall, there was originally a full-length masculine figure; this was removed at an indeterminate date, though the legs are still just visible in a lower layer of paint. The general appearance of this personage, who is known from copies and from other versions done in Snyders' studio, is that of a man holding the head of a wild boar; or (though less probably) it may be a fisherman emptying a basin of fish, as in a painting quite similar to this one (now in the North Carolina Museum in Raleigh).
V.D.

Anthony van Dyck
Antwerp, 1599 - London, 1641

Two Studies of Heads
Oil on paper mounted on wood
0.49 x 0.58
Loaned by the State, 1811
Inv. A 119

Van Dyck seems to have been introduced to the practice of studies of heads in Rubens's studio, where he went to work in 1615-1616 (or perhaps before then). It was not only a case of studying an interesting physiognomy from life, and as seen from different angles, but also a question of constituting a stock of models which could then be used in the execution of a major composition. Thus the head on the left appears as one of the apostles in *Christ Suffers the Children to Come unto Him*, in the National Gallery of Ontario, Ottawa.

But the two heads shown here should above all be seen as corresponding to the half-length apostles painted during the artist's stay in Antwerp, or afterwards. These were sometimes in the form of complete sets of twelve figures, which have now been broken up and (with one exception) are difficult to reconstitute, or to classify chronologically. The head on the left of the sketch is identical to that of *The Apostle Simon*, leaning on his saw (Kunsthistorisches Museum, Vienna), while that on the right corresponds to *The Apostle Philip* (ditto), carrying a cross, his eyes raised towards heaven.

This sketch, painted in an exalted style, at once light and rough, is a good example of the expressive and dramatic power of Van Dyck's art.

V.D.

**Jan Brueghel the Elder,
called "Velvet Brueghel"**
Brussels, 1568 - Antwerp, 1625

Fire
1606
Oil on wood
0.46 x 0.83
Loaned by the State, 1811
Inv. A 75

In 1605, Brueghel began a set of four paintings of identical format for his Milanese protector and patron, Cardinal Borromeo. The theme was the four elements, and Brueghel took sixteen years to complete the set, which is now divided up between the Pinacoteca Ambrosiana in Milan (*Fire* and *Water*) and the Louvre in Paris (*Air* and *Earth*). In parallel with this first version of the four elements, Brueghel was thinking about a second one, which he himself copied, as well as having large numbers of copies made in his studio. Certain sets of this second version are complete, like the one in Lyon, which comes from the celebrated collection of the Archduke Leopold Wilhelm of Austria, Regent of the Netherlands, and which is particularly important, not only in terms of its very high quality, but also on account of the fact that three of its four panels are dated (*Fire*, 1606; *Earth*, 1610; *Air*, 1611). Whereas three of the compositions are organised around a female figure placed in the centre of an Edenesque landscape (Ceres, in *Earth*, and two allegorical figures in *Air* and *Water*), *Fire* takes up once again the traditional representation of Venus in Vulcan's forge, which in this case is a pretext for a detailed description of metalworking in all its forms, a sort of encyclopædia of human arts and techniques, on a background of ancient ruins inspired by the Palatine hill in Rome.

A recent restoration of these panels has made it possible to get a better idea of the creative process which informed such works: the pentimenti, which are numerous, and the notations of details which seem to develop, to be superimposed on one another and to interlink to infinity, allow free rein to a poetic imagination that is refined and virtuoso, far removed from any repetitive, mechanical procedure.
V.D.

Jacob van Loo
Sluis, 1614 - Paris, 1670

Young Woman Going to Bed
("Le Coucher à l'italienne")
c. 1650
Oil on canvas
1.87 x 1.43
Acquired in 1941
Inv. 1941-5

It is difficult, at present, to imagine the extraordinary reputation that this painting achieved in the 18th century and the start of the 19th. It was acquired in 1815 for a very high price by the neo-classical sculptor Jean-Baptiste Giraud (1752-1830) — who was best known for his private collection of mouldings of ancient sculptures — and remained thereafter in the hands of his family. It was almost forgotten until its purchase by the museum of Lyon during the Second World War.

The reputation of the work was, of course, a result of the subject — a representation, almost life-size, of a female nude, unrelated to any historical or mythological context — as well as the price it fetched in certain sales, more than the intrinsic qualities of the painting itself, real as they may be (for example in the splendid detail of the cloth thrown over the table), though indeed it is true that van Loo gave a more refined treatment to his small-format nudes.

The artist appears to have derived his inspiration, in this case, from a painting by Jordaens, *King Candaules Shows his Wife to Gyges*, painted before 1646 (Nationalmuseum, Stockholm), where the king's spouse appears in the foreground, preparing to enter her bed, in an almost identical pose and situation to the one seen here. Did van Loo intend to suggest, with a certain irony, that the viewer should identify with Gyges or Candaules? Or was it simply a case of a subject featuring a "courtesan", which was a frequent theme in Northern painting after the 16th century (though, admittedly, rarely in a state of undress)? Whatever the initial intention may have been, there remains the audacity of a composition whose eroticism is direct and novel, and whose fascination for the artists of the 18th century is easy to understand.
V.D.

Abraham van Beyeren
The Hague, 1620-1621
Overschie, 1690

*Silver Cup, Lemon, Grapes
and Watch*
Oil on wood
0.75 x 0.60
Acquired in 1852
Inv. A 2855

Van Beyeren was essentially a painter of still lifes,
multiplying their themes and diversifying his
output. He favoured sumptuous displays,
reflecting the influence of Jan Davidsz de Heem
(1606-1683/4), but also still lifes with fish, fruit
and, as here, small banquets of an almost austere
appearance. He is also known for hunting scenes,
bouquets of flowers, and a number of seascapes.
The opulence of the silver cup, with its admirable
reflections, the play of light on the precious
stemmed glass, and the fleshy tenderness of the grapes and the bread, should
not be allowed to mislead us: the open watch and the spiral of the lemon
skin are there to recall the flow of time and the vanity of all things, and to
encourage abstemiousness in the spectator.
V.D.

Jan van Noordt
Amsterdam, c. 1623-1624
(?), 1676 or later

Full-length Portrait of a Boy
1665
Oil on canvas
1.570 x 1.225
Acquired in 1897
Inv. B 577

Jan van Noordt was born into a family of musicians in Amsterdam, where he seems to have spent his entire career (though indeed little is known of his life). He belonged to the same artistic circle as Jacob van Loo (cf. N° 124), which was also that of the historical painters who were students of Jacob Becker (1608-1651). His most distinctive feature is his tortured, baroque forms, which gives him something in common with the Flemish painters.

In this portrait of a child, whose identity is unknown, the influence of Van Dyck is manifest in the elegance of the presentation, and features such as the column, the heavy drapings and the crepuscular landscape. But the congenial appearance of the model, and the gesture of greeting to the spectator, are examples of van Noordt's more personal touches.
V.D.

Jan Davidsz de Heem
Utrecht, 1606 - Antwerp, 1683-1684

Garland of Flowers and
Fruit, with a Portrait of
William III of Orange
c. 1661-1672
Oil on canvas
1.34 x 1.14
Loaned by the State, 1811
Inv. A 85

According to A. Houbraken, this painting was commissioned from de Heem by the Utrecht painter Johan van der Meer, who may have presented it to William III (1650-1702) in 1672, in the hope of obtaining a position. That year, while the armies of Louis XIV were invading Holland, a popular uprising brought the young prince William III, the son of William II of Orange (1626-1650) and Mary II Stuart (1631-1660), to the stadtholdership. This tumultuous political context underlies the rich symbolism of the canvas: the red and white roses under the portrait make reference to the houses of Lancaster and York, from which the mother of the prince was descended. The lion of the Netherlands holds an orange, which recalls the rights of the family over the principality of Orange, further indicated by the orange sash across the bust. As to the two eagles holding the horns of plenty, they are signs of sovereignty. The portrait itself, which is undoubtedly the work of another hand, takes up once more a prototype executed in 1661 by the painter Abraham Ragineau.

De Heem's composition follows the Flemish tradition of floral garlands, notably perfected by Daniel Seghers and Adrian van Utrecht in Antwerp, where the artist spent the major part of his career. The canvas shown here is among the most accomplished of the genre: it was sent to Lyon by Napoleon's administration in 1811, and represents a notable contribution to the effort made to bring together in Lyon high-quality paintings of flowers as models for the revival of the silk industry.

V.D.

Michiel Jansz van Miereveld
Delft, 1567 - 1641

Portrait of a Woman
1625
Oil on wood
1.13 x 0.85
Acquired between 1808 and 1813
Inv. A 111

The identity of this 28-year-old woman with the fine, pale face, set in an extraordinary lace ruff, remains unknown. Somewhat frozen in the sumptuousness of her dress, she is facing to the right, as tradition required, towards her spouse, whose portrait, which has disappeared, would presumably have provided a counterpart to her own. The painter's palette, which is as restrained as the sartorial mode demanded, plays ably with the opposition of blacks and whites, and modulates with skill the golds and greys. This work constitutes an epitome of the art of Miereveld, who was the favourite painter of the Dutch aristocracy and upper classes in the first quarter of the 17th century, and whose considerable output was kept up by his international reputation and by the efficient organisation of a studio to which was entrusted the painting of the garments.
V.D.

Rembrandt Harmensz van Rijn
Leyden, 1606 - Amsterdam, 1669

The Lapidation of St Stephen
1625
Oil on wood
0.89 x 1.23
Acquired in 1844
Inv. A 2735

This *Lapidation of St Stephen,* rediscovered in 1962 in the museum's reserves, and dated 1625, is the first known work by Rembrandt. Aged 19 or 20 at the time, the artist was still under the influence of the historical painter Pieter Lastman (*c.* 1583-1633), with whom he had worked for several months in Amsterdam around 1623-1624, and whose manner, at once narrative, expansive and realist, can be clearly distinguished in this painting.

The subject, which is drawn from the *Acts of the Apostles* (Chapters 6 and 7), recounts the martyrdom of this young deacon of the Christian community in Jerusalem, who was unjustly put to death for blasphemy as a result of false testimony. The instant chosen is that when Stephen, kneeling, invokes the Lord before meeting his fate. In the centre of the background is Saul, seated, with the cloaks of the lapidators on his knees. The violently expressive style that is seen in the gestures and faces, and the highly accentuated effects of light, are the central characteristics of Rembrandt's first Leyden years. The way in which the heads are made to fill up every empty space might certainly be judged a little awkward, but there is already, in the powerful diagonal which traverses the composition, and from which springs up the body of an executioner, all the audacious inventiveness of a great master.
V.D.

Jan van Bylert
Utrecht, *c.* 1597-1598 - 1671

The Go-between
c. 1625-1630
Oil on canvas
1.03 x 1.54
Loaned by the State, 1803
Inv. A 25

As a genre painter, portraitist and historical painter, Jan van Bylert was a member of the Caravaggian school in Utrecht. Like Honthorst, Ter Brugghen and Baburen, he learnt the lessons of Caravaggio and his immediate disciples in Italy; then, on his return to Utrecht — a town which was marked by a strong Catholic and ultramontane tradition — he contributed, with them, to the definition and propagation of a northern European version of Caravaggism. His personal style was strongly marked by classicism; but his figures progressively adopted a style which, by comparison, was calmer and smoother, and whose colours were lighter and colder.

This *Go-between* is nonetheless a youthful work, no doubt painted during the years which immediately followed van Bylert's return to Utrecht, in 1624. It possesses all the "picaresque" verve and freshness of scenes featuring courtesans, gamblers and bohemians, often represented half-length in order to render the effect on the spectator more immediate. The description of this shady world, with its slightly facile picturesqueness, was intended to be at once satirical and moralising: the theme of the young dupe is combined with that of the confrontation between old age and youth, and the resulting idea of vanity. V.D.

Salomon Koninck
Amsterdam, 1609 - 1656

Manoah's Sacrifice
c. 1650
Oil on canvas
2.62 x 2.32
Gift of cardinal Fesch, 1816
Inv. A 204

This monumental composition — which is in fact the largest known painting by Salomon Koninck — eloquently expresses the ambition of Dutch artists in the field of historical painting, who on this point, contrary to an idea that is still too widespread, yielded nothing to their colleagues of the southern Netherlands. Koninck, in particular, had a taste for pomp and magnificence. Thus, for the theme (which was frequently illustrated in Rembrandt's entourage) of the annunciation of the birth of Samson to Manoah and his wife, who was sterile, he chose a theatrical illustration of two young personages, in sumptuous costume, rather than the traditional iconography of a man and a woman, already old, in simple dress. The angel himself, who is about to disappear into the flames of the sacrifice — thus bringing Manoah to an understanding of the divine message — participates in Koninck's love of rich cloth with changing highlights, as well as his taste for declamatory gestures.

The fascinating, strange gold object which gleams softly in the foreground further reinforces the supernatural impression: it is a vase which was made in 1614 by Adam van Vianen (c. 1569-1627) for the goldsmiths' guild in Amsterdam, and which is to be seen in numerous historical paintings.
V.D.

Gerard Terborch the Younger

Zwolle, 1617 - Deventer, 1681

Lady Reading a Letter Before a Messenger
c. 1658-1660
Oil on canvas
0.51 x 0.38
Acquired in 1820
Inv. A 109

In 17th century Dutch genre painting, the theme of the letter was almost always associated with that of love. For the spectator of the time, a lady writing or receiving a letter would quite naturally suggest a romantic correspondence, especially when, as in this instance, a mirror, or some toiletry articles left lying on a table, accentuated the suggestion. And it is possible that, as was often the case, this painting had a counterpart showing a man writing a letter, which may in fact be the composition known as the *Officer Dictating a Letter,* a work that has survived only in the form of copies, the best of which is in the Alte Meister Gemäldegalerie in Dresden.

Most of Terborch's interiors, depicting personages of polite — or not-so-polite — Dutch society, were painted during the decade which followed his moving to Deventer in 1654. This work, with its unity and harmony, and the extreme delicacy with which the nuances of light in the room are conveyed, is habitually considered to date from the end of the 1650s, which was the painter's mature period.

V.D.

**Gerrit Adriaensz.
Berckheyde**
Haarlem, 1638 - 1698

*The Great Market of
Haarlem, in front of Saint
Bavon's Church*
1673
Oil on wood
0.42 x 0.62
Acquired in 1890
Inv. B 446

Gerrit Berckheyde was, with Van der Heyden, the best known of the Dutch architectural painters; both of them specialised in urban views. He applied himself mostly to depicting Haarlem, his home town, but also painted scenes in Amsterdam and The Hague.

From the middle of the 1660s onwards, Berckheyde did several representations of the market square in Haarlem, from different angles. Here the viewpoint is situated close to the facade of the town hall, the columns of whose peristyle, now destroyed, can be seen on the left.

Berckheyde's compositions are always dominated by a principal monument, in this case the Gothic church dedicated to the patron saint of the city, Saint Bavon, which was completed in 1538. Around the square, which is the site of the meat market, the gabled houses and the fish market are described in detail, as well as the human figures, which appear strangely immobile. This urban landscape seems to sum up the social life of Haarlem in the 17th century, with the symbolic presence of the different powers: political, religious and economic. It is possible that a view from the opposite side, dating from the same year (and which is now in the Hermitage in Saint Petersburg), constitutes a matching piece to this one.

As always with this artist, the palette is restricted, with a preponderance of grey and beige tints, marked contrasts between zones of shadow and brightness, and coldness of light.
V.D.

Paul Mignard
Avignon, 1641 - Lyon, 1691

Portrait of Nicolas Mignard
1672
Oil on canvas
1.59 x 1.26
Loaned by the State, 1803
Inv. A 56

This is the competition piece that Paul Mignard presented on 11 June 1672 at the royal academy of painting and sculpture. In this work the artist (who is less well known than his uncle, Pierre Mignard, Louis XIV's official painter) pays tribute to his father, a painter from Avignon (d. 1668). Paul Mignard, who was essentially a portraitist, settled down in Lyon in 1689, and the following year was given the title of "ordinary painter of the city of Lyon".

Nicolas Mignard is represented here painting with his left hand, which is biographically accurate. He is probably executing one of his last compositions, namely an *Annunciation* (whose fate is unknown) which had been commissioned by Louis XIV in 1667 for the oratory of his apartments on the ground floor of the Tuileries in Paris. The preparatory drawing for the figure of the Virgin, attached to the stretcher, and a study for drapings placed on the table, are there as aids to the artist. Some scholarly accessories, such as the compass and Palladio's treatise on architecture, speak of the painter's erudition. Paul had to make use of a *Self-Portrait* by Nicolas, doubtless the one that is now in the Musée Calvet in Avignon, which he rendered more youthful in order to produce this likeness, whose sobriety and depth are impressive.
V.D.

Alexandre François Desportes
Champigneulles, 1661 - Paris, 1743

Still Life with Peacock
1714
Oil on canvas
2.05 x 1.80
Loaned by the State, 1799
Inv. A 54

This painting, which was executed for the décor of the Duke d'Antin's mansion in Paris, has a matching piece, *Game, Fruit and Dog before a Balustrade* (Angers, Musée des Beaux-Arts). Here Desportes demonstrates his knowledge of how to produce a skilful blend of classical architecture and a landscape with foliage, along with sculpture and still-life subjects. The balustrade, which divides the painting into two almost equal parts, gives it a theatrical appearance which is reinforced by the heavy red drapes. The bas-reliefs, which are inspired by the style of the sculptor François Duquesnoy, represent centaurs carrying off young women. Various animals, like the monkey and the macaw, introduce the exotic note which is habitual to this kind of décor. The rendering of the materials, the silkiness of the fabrics, the transparency of the grapes, and the treatment of the monkey's coat and the peacock's plumage, reveal the northern origins of the artist's influences.
V.D.

Joseph Vivien
Lyon, 1657 - Bonn, 1734

Self-Portrait
c. 1715-1720
Oil on canvas
1.16 x 0.84
Acquired in 1994
Inv. 1994-1

Joseph Vivien, who was a brilliant student of Charles Le Brun and was received into the academy in 1701, left Lyon in 1672 and spent most of his career abroad. He lived mainly in Munich, where he was appointed official painter to the Elector Maximilian Emmanuel of Bavaria, Governor of the Netherlands.

Vivien was a dazzling pastellist, which earned him the nickname of "the century's Van Dyck of the pastel"; he initiated the fashion for portraits using this medium, which enjoyed great popularity throughout the 18th century. Several self-portraits in pastel are known, and a lesser number in oils; all are treated with panache. The artist's pose is elegant, and shows him to advantage, depicting him in front of what would appear to be a huge allegorical composition on the theme of *The Reunion of Maximilian Emmanuel of Bavaria with his Family* (Munich, Alte Pinakothek), which he had begun in 1715 and which he finished only in 1733, a year before his death. The shimmering beauty of the fabrics, the refinement of the purple and saffron tones, and the acuity of the psychological study make this canvas a veritable manifesto of the art of the portrait at the beginning of the 18th century.
V.D.

Jean-François de Troy

Paris, 1679 - Rome, 1752

The Judgement of Solomon

1742

Oil on canvas

1.91 x 1.43

Acquired in 1952

Inv. 1952-2

This painting, and the one beside it, *Jesus and the Samaritan Woman*, were commissioned from Jean-François de Troy by Cardinal de Tencin in 1742; de Troy was at that time the director of the French Academy in Rome. The cardinal, who had been made archbishop of Lyon in 1740, did not take up his duties there until July 1742, on his return from a long voyage to Rome, where he met the painter. There were four other compositions in the cycle, which was intended for a gallery of paintings in the archdiocesan palace on the banks of the river Saône. The themes were paired: two were drawn from Roman history, two from the Old Testament and two from the New. Of the six, it is only the two which are now in Lyon whose whereabouts are known.

In a cramped frame, where the action seems to be piled up onto itself, a knot of figures, whose gestures are highly demonstrative, give violent expression to their emotions. A great diagonal divides the painting into two opposing parts: Solomon and his counsellors are in the shadows, while the executioner and the women are in the full glare of the light. The sincere, successful pathos of this coloured tableau shows the heights that historical painting could still reach in the middle of the 18th century, just a short time before the reforms began, and before the new ambitions of the end of Louis XV's reign came to a head.

V.D.

Bernardo Bellotto
Venice, 1721 - Warsaw, 1780

The Grand Canal, Venice
c. 1736-1740
Oil on canvas
0.79 x 1.21
Acquired in 1890
Inv. B 472

In 1735, Bernardo Bellotto entered the studio of his uncle, Antonio Canal ("Canaletto"), the celebrated painter of panoramic views of Venice. This speciality, known as the "veduta", which was very popular in the 18th century, was encouraged by the ever-increasing demand produced by the voyagers who were already coming to Venice in large numbers. The Grand Canal is depicted here in its upper reaches, at the level of the Campo San Samuele. On the right is a disparate group of houses which were demolished to make way for the Palazzo Grassi, built by Giorgio Massari starting in 1748-1749. In the background, the Palazzo Balbi is recognisable, with its two obelisks on the roof. Behind it, framing it almost symmetrically, is the campanile of the church of the Frari, on the left, and the belfry of the San Toma church, on the right. On the left, the Ca' Rezzonico for the moment consists of no more than a ground floor and a first floor, built by Baldassare Longhena, with a provisional covering to protect the building from the elements. The second floor and top floor were only constructed (by Giorgio Massari) in the period between 1752 and 1756.

Bellotto went even further than Canaletto in his concern for topographical veracity. But this apparent exactitude was not antagonistic to poetic expression: here, the beauty of the atmospheric light illuminates buildings whose walls have been eaten away by the water, as well as gleaming palazzos. The nautical ballet of the gondolas and the small coloured figures, a little naive, are picturesque anecdotes which add life to this architectural painting.

V.D.

François Boucher
Paris, 1703 - 1770

The Light of the World
1750
Oil on canvas
1.75 x 1.30
Loaned by the Louvre, 1955
Inv. 1955-106

This painting was intended for the decoration of the altar of Madame de Pompadour's private chapel in her château at Bellevue. The chapel in question was in fact an antichamber that could serve as an oratory when one left open the doors of the small space containing the altar, above which was placed the painting. This fact explains the dimensions of the work, which is smaller than those generally used for retables.

The painting itself marks an essential stage in Boucher's career: not only was it one of Madame de Pompadour's first commissions, but it was also the first large-scale religious work produced by the artist, who was not very active in this genre (only five such works being known). A short time after this particular canvas was exhibited in the Salon of 1750, the artist obtained lodgings at the Louvre, and also the position of First Painter to the king.

The subject represented is not strictly speaking a Nativity (given the presence of personages who are foreign to the scene, and the absence of the donkey). Nor is it an adoration of the shepherds, given that there are no sheep, and that the man on the right, with his hat and his gourd, resembles a pilgrim. The real subject is in fact that of the title given by Fessard's 1761 engraving, *The Light of the World*, the light which this birth brings to the entire human race — children, adults and old people — and which, piercing the clouds, puts the divine world in communication with terrestrial realities, as symbolised by the hen and the eggs in the foreground. The way in which this light is treated, the way in which it radiates in a halo around the child, softening the forms and melting into the clouds, shows that Boucher had heeded the lessons of the Italian masters, and particularly those of Correggio.
V.D.

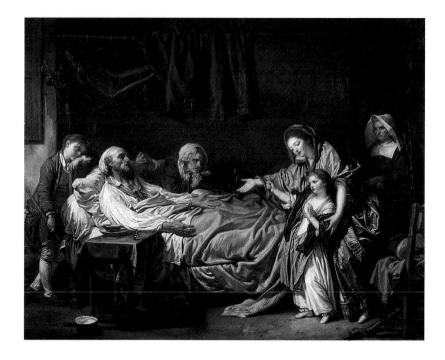

Jean-Baptiste Greuze
Tournus, 1725 - Paris, 1805

The Lady of Charity
c. 1772-1775
Oil on canvas
1.12 x 1.46
Acquired in 1897
Inv. B 576

The date of this painting remains uncertain. Greuze exhibited it in his studio in 1775, at the time of the Salon at the Louvre in which, in opposition to the Academy, he refused to participate, and from which he was absent up to 1800. In 1772 Jean Massard had published an engraving which gave the essential details of the composition, below a medallion showing the face of the "lady of charity" (to whom Greuze in fact lent the features of his wife, Gabrielle Babuti).

This is the first important painting done by the artist after the scandal caused by his *Septimus Severus* in 1769. It was also his first "moral painting" in contemporary costume, and the critics — notably Diderot — covered it with eulogies. It portrays a young woman of comfortable means showing her daughter a spectacle of poverty and suffering, and teaching her charity by making her give a purse to a sick person, despite the child's unwillingness. The influence of Poussin is clear in this case: the frieze-like composition, and the role given to the bed and the curtain, are direct references, as is the importance accorded to the gestures and faces in the expression of feelings. Certain details shed light on the scene in a symbolic way, and the sword hung above the bed indicates unequivocally that the poor, sick person is in fact a nobleman.
V.D.

Jean-Jacques de Boissieu
Lyon, 1736 - 1810

Animal Market
Oil on canvas
0.53 x 0.73
Acquired in 1834
Inv. A 97

Jean-Jacques de Boissieu was a self-taught painter of landscapes and scenes from everyday life. His painted works are few in number by comparison with his sketches and engravings; in fact only about twenty canvases are known, all of them executed between 1765 and 1780. His art shared in the general enthusiasm of his age for the northern European painting of the 17th century, and this contributed to his success among art-lovers.

Here the artist represents the suburbs of Lyon on a market day, apparently juxtaposing the church of Charbonnières and the gates of the village of Ambronnay. In the same way, he brings together in a slightly artificial way several picturesque little scenes composed of human figures and animals, depicting them painstakingly and in great detail. A restricted range of colours contributes to the feeling of calm which emanates from the composition. The fine, smooth, porcelained touch is another sign of the influence of Dutch painting on de Boissieu's art.

V.D.

Étienne-Maurice Falconet
Paris, 1716 - 1791

*Doctor Camille Falconet
(1671-1762)*
1747
Terracotta
H. 0.54; L. 0.30; Depth 0.25
Loaned by the Town Library,
Lyon, 1904
Inv. B 675

As seems to be indicated by an inscription in Greek on the back of this bust ("Of the two namesakes, one has reproduced the other by artistic means; the younger has represented the elder"), Dr Falconet, who was the King's medical consultant, as well as a distinguished bibliophile and a founder of the Academy of Lyon, does not seem to have been a relation of the other, younger Falconet, who was however a friend of his. This superb bust, which shows the continued influence of Jean-Baptiste II Lemoyne (who for a long time was Falconet's teacher), represents the doctor at the age of 77. Wearing a voluminous wig and a simple shirt with an open neck, the old man presents an open countenance, attentively and realistically modelled in the minutest detail. The artist sent this bust to the Salon in 1747, and 13 years later exhibited a second version, in marble, showing the doctor without a wig; this latter work is now in the Musée des Beaux-Arts in Angers.
C.B.

Jean-Baptiste II Lemoyne
Paris, 1704 - 1778

*Bernard Le Bovier
de Fontenelle (1657-1757)*
1748
Terracotta
H. 0.59; L. 0.36; Depth 0.26
Gift of Charles Gillet's heirs, 1974
Inv. 1974-4

As a particularly prolific portraitist at the court of Louis XV, where he was the official sculptor, Lemoyne exhibited several busts at the Salon of 1748: along with those of Voltaire, de la Tour and Mademoiselle de Bonnac there was this terracotta portrait of Fontenelle. Lemoyne gave one version of the work to the Académie des Arts in Rouen in 1759, and the terracotta original to the Académie des Sciences in Paris in 1771. The one shown here may be a version that was mentioned in an auction in 1782. Modelled with virtuosity, it is distinguished by the high quality of its execution. The artist has succeeded in rendering, at one and the same time, the congenial personality of his model — the author of *Conversations on the Plurality of Worlds* — and his vivacity of spirit as a skilled populariser of science and a precursor of the Enlightenment philosophers.
C.B.

Louis-Claude Vassé
Paris, 1716 - 1772

Young Boy Wearing a Turban
1759
Marble
H. 0.46; L. 0.30; Depth 0.18
Mr and Mrs Fitler Bequest, 1926
Inv. B 1389

"Vassé's greatest claim to glory is perhaps the truly exquisite collection of his busts of children — his 'bambinelli' (as he called them) — which prefigured, and sometimes equalled, Houdon's delightful child portraits": such was Louis Réau's judgement, and it might be applied in particular to this charming head of a little boy, full of life and gaiety, whose model, it has recently been suggested, may have been the only son of the sculptor Pierre-Louis Vassé. Dated 1759 on the plinth, this bust was probably exhibited in the Salon that same year; two other, later, versions in marble are known of, which suggests that a certain success was achieved by the work, where the virtuosity of the treatment of the locks of hair and the folds of the turban does not stifle the sincerity of the study of the facial features.
V.D.

Jean-Antoine Houdon
Versailles, 1741 - Paris, 1828

Bust of a Young Girl
Plaster
H. 0.59; L. 0,34; Depth 0,21
Acquired in 1995
Inv. 1995-9

Houdon presented his portraits of children in the Salon from 1777 onwards. They were the most accomplished expressions of the late 18th century's penchant for the theme of childhood (Jean-Jacques Rousseau's *Emile* appeared in 1762). They constitute one of the most justly famous components of his work. This bust of an anonymous little girl of around 12 may have figured among several "heads of children", including that of his daughter Sabine (Louvre, Paris), which were exhibited in the Salon of 1791, the date inscribed on a marble version that is now in the Australian National Gallery in Canberra. The plaster version shown here bears the stamp of the studio, and is striking in terms of the quality of its execution and the fineness of its modelling, as well as its intact surface, on which still appear some marks of final touches; this latter feature shows that it was used as a model. The highly distinctive technique of the treatment of the pupil, the discreet fleshy realism of the nascent breast and the virtuosity of the locks of hair, not forgetting the delicately dreamy expression in the eyes, exemplify the style of Houdon at his best.
V.D.

Paintings and Sculptures
19th and 20th centuries
Rooms 14 to 31

Joseph Chinard
Lyon, 1756 - 1813

Juliette Récamier
1805 or 1806
Marble
H. 0.80; L. 0.42; Depth 0,30
Acquired in 1909
Inv. B 871

"Seen face-on, it shows a modest reserve, in keeping with the graceful, almost childlike pose... in profile, with different nuances, the pert nose with its slightly drawn-back nostrils and the suggestion of a smile floating over the lips express a *je ne sais quoi* of piquancy, if not provocation, accentuated by the transparent scarf, the throat and the exposed breast". It was thus that Édouard Herriot described the ambiguous, but very real, charm of Chinard's most celebrated work, which is also one of the finest portraits of Juliette Récamier at the height of her beauty, executed some years before the no less celebrated painting by Baron Gérard (1805), which is in the Carnavalet museum. It was probably during one of his visits to Paris, in 1801 or 1802, when he stayed with the Récamiers, that Chinard executed the clay model for this marble bust, which he sculpted in Carrara in 1805 or 1806.

P.D.

Antonio Canova
Possagno, 1757 - Venice, 1822

The Three Graces
1810
Terracotta
H. 0.42; L. 0.25; Depth 0.12
Juliette Récamier Bequest, 1849
Inv. H 794

This terracotta piece, which is of exceptional sensitivity, is the only original maquette by Canova to be found in a French public collection. On 9 November 1810, Canova paid a visit to the former Empress Josephine at Malmaison. Was it on this occasion that the project for a commission of a group illustrating the theme of the "Three Graces" took shape? If one may believe the inscription and the date on this piece, Canova had already come up with the general idea for this composition before his journey to France (he did not return to Rome until the end of December). Josephine's definitive commission dates from 13 June 1813, and the full-size plaster model, which is now in Possagno, was made between June and August of that same year. Josephine, who died the following year, never saw the final marble version, which was completed in 1816. It passed into the hands of Eugène de Beauharnais, and is now in the Hermitage in Saint Petersburg. The exact circumstances in which Juliette Récamier took possession of this work are not known: it may have been during her meeting with Canova in 1813.
P.D.

Antoine Berjon
Lyon, 1754 - 1843

Fruit and Flowers
in a Wicker Basket
1810
Oil on canvas
1.07 x 0.87
Acquired in 1811
Inv. A 181

This monumental still life is one of Berjon's most highly "composed" bouquets, and shows, most particularly, his debt to the great northern European tradition. It is the only one of the Musée de Lyon's large collection of Berjon's works to have been acquired during the artist's lifetime; it was exhibited by François Artaud, the curator of the museum at that time, in the "Salon de la Fleur", along with Bony, Daël, Huysum, Mignon, Desportes and Monnoyer, whose works were to contribute to the training of textile designers at La Fabrique; flower painting, which played such an important role in the artistic life of Lyon in the 19th century, was in effect intimately linked to the silk industry. This painting, which was no doubt exhibited in the Paris Salon of 1810, is one of Berjon's last "Parisian" works; it was painted a short time before his return to his native Lyon and his appointment as head of the "Flower" class at the École des Beaux-Arts.

D.B.

Jean-Michel Grobon

Lyon, 1770 - 1853

The Former Pêcherie Quarter in Lyon

Oil on wood

0.29 x 0.50

Paul Grand Bequest, 1891

Inv. B 486

This faithful depiction of a district of Lyon which has now disappeared is of undeniable documentary interest. It constitutes, above all, the most accomplished demonstration of the qualities possessed by the founder of the Lyon school of painting. With a precision of treatment very similar to that of the minor Dutch masters of the 17th century, Grobon, who lived near the quarter represented here, and knew it well, omits not a single paving-stone from the Place de la Feuillée, in the foreground, nor any detail of the facades with their painted signs, half blotted out. The narrow street traversed by a ray of sunlight was to become the Quai de la Pêcherie, after the destruction of the large house on the waterside, dominated by the square tower of its staircase. In the background there is the Ainay district, behind the Pont du Change, which crosses the river Saône in the middle distance.

The delicacy of the colouring and the enamelled appearance of the execution add to the nostalgic feeling which emanates from this small *veduta*, which is bathed in a lustrous light, bringing to life an age that is now past and gone.

C.B.

Pierre Révoil
Lyon, 1776 - Paris, 1842

The Tournament of Rennes
1812
Oil on canvas
1.33 x 1.74
Gift of the artist, 1839
Inv. A 164

Exhibited in the Salon of 1812, this painting illustrates, in a particularly characteristic way, the Troubadour style, which was known as the "anecdotal genre" by contemporary commentators, and which drew its themes mostly from medieval history. Révoil was the main representative of this current, along with Fleury-Richard, another of David's students from Lyon. As an erudite painter, and an early collector of medieval art objects, he undertakes here a painstaking archæological reconstruction of the minutest details of the Tournament of Rennes, which saw the participation, in an anonymous suit of armour, of the young Bertrand Duguesclin, in defiance of his father's order. Révoil chose to represent this moment when, after Bertrand's triumph over his numerous adversaries, the last of the vanquished raises the victor's visor. The herald in the foreground is sounding the victory, while in the background one of the four judges holds aloft the prize for the joust, a silver swan. As regards décor, costumes, accessories, coats of arms, and even the motto written on the stands, the artist has left nothing to the imagination.
C.B.

Fleury Richard
Lyon, 1777 - Écully, 1852

Madame Elisabeth of France, the King's Sister
1816
Oil on canvas
0.690 x 0.905
Acquired with the help of the
F.R.A.M., 1988
Inv. 1988-4.III.5

Painted a year after a larger version which was exhibited in the 1817 Salon (Musée National du Château, Versailles), this work, which is one of Fleury-Richard's masterpieces, is perfectly in keeping with certain Restoration painters' concern to rehabilitate the royal family by bringing their virtues to the forefront. Madame Elisabeth, the sister of Louis XVI, met with the same unhappy fate as her brother. Here, she is attending a distribution of milk at her property in Montreuil. This open-air scene marks a departure from the interiors in the Dutch taste which had up to that time made the artist's name. The composition makes good use of the contrast between the back-lighting of the foreground and the warm, oblique light that illuminates the figures in the middle ground. The pillars of the creamery clearly separate the composition into three distinct scenes: on the right, the cow being milked, in the centre the distribution of the milk, on the left Elisabeth, mixing with the village children. The sensitivity of the play of light expresses the delicacy of the sentiments of the benefactress, whose luminous parasol takes on the appearance of a halo.
C.B.

Antoine-Jean Duclaux
Lyon, 1783 - 1868

Lyon Artists Stopping Off at the Île Barbe
1824
Oil on canvas
0.86 x 1.31
Acquired in 1825
Inv. A 142

Duclaux was a landscape and animal painter. In this work he represents several of his colleagues — who, like him, were students of Révoil — during an outing in the country. Grouped around Fleury-Richard are the painters Genod, Thierriat, Trimolet, Jacomin, Bonnefond and Rey, and the sculptor Legendre-Héral. The Île Barbe, whose tip can be seen on the left of the painting, is situated in the river Saône north of Lyon. The artists shown here were particularly fond of it, and painted it often. In this harmonious landscape, which is bathed in summer light, the artist skilfully varies the poses of his friends — these well-dressed young men mixing the pleasures of the outing with the business of searching out picturesque landscapes.

In exhibiting this group portrait at the Paris Salon of 1824, Duclaux was putting forward a veritable manifesto of the ambitions of the young Lyon school, which for some years previously had been marked by its interest in genre painting, served by painstaking technique.

C.B.

French school
c. 1795

The Market Gardener
Oil on paper mounted on canvas
0.82 x 0.65
Gift of Thierry Bröelmann, 1861
Inv. A 2932

This painting is undoubtedly one of the museum's most famous. Originally, and for a considerable period of time, it was attributed to David, due to its high pictorial quality; but this attribution has now been given up, and numerous other names have been suggested: Greuze, Vincent, the Lyonnais artist Berjon, and indeed Géricault, Gros, or even Delacroix.

As a symbol of a woman of the people of Paris during the Revolution — in Focillon's words "the portrait of a class, of a time, of their sombre virtues" — this portrait remains striking in terms of the power of its realism and the acuity of its expression. Everything in the figure is expressive of a challenge: the head held high, the fierce eye, the mouth half-open, the arms crossed. And the sense of revolt is further reinforced by the red and brown tones. The rapidity of execution, well served by a flowing technique, contributes to the spirited quality of the image. The folds in the clothes are treated summarily, but the face reveals a particular fineness, with a concern for the rendering of the weatherbeaten wrinkles and the sparse hair.
V.D.

Pierre-Paul Prud'hon
Cluny, 1758 - Paris, 1823

*Madame Anthony
and Her Sons*
1796
Oil on canvas
0.98 x 0.81
Acquired in 1892
Inv. B 493

At the end of 1794, Prud'hon, fleeing revolutionary Paris, settled in Franche Comté. It was apparently as the result of an incident that took place along the way, at Rigny, near Gray, that he was forced to accept the hospitality of a family in the region. During his stay in the Haute Saône region, where he remained until 1796, the artist painted a large number of portraits, though none compares with that of Mme Anthony, a masterpiece whose charm is free of all sentimentality, a miracle of emotion and frankness. Mme Anthony was born Louise Demandre; she married Georges Anthony, the postmaster of Arc les Gray, in 1790. Here she is seen holding her son Joseph, who is dressed in the fashion of the time and is standing on a table; her elder son Frédi is standing behind her. The matching portrait, showing her husband standing beside his horse, is in the Musée des Beaux-Arts in Dijon.

C.B.

François Gérard
Rome, 1770 - Paris, 1837

Corinne at Cape Misène
1819-1821
Oil on canvas
2.565 x 2.770
Juliette Récamier Bequest, 1849
Inv. A 2840

This celebrated work was commissioned in April 1819 by Prince Augustus of Prussia from Baron Gérard, through Madame Récamier, to pay tribute to Madame de Staël, who had died two years before, and whose novel, *Corinne*, provided the subject of the painting. It was suggested by the prince himself, who asked the painter to represent the heroine with "the embellished features of Madame de Staël". The scene is that in which the poetess Corinne, having evoked the memories attached to the famous site, interrupts her improvisation and, overcome by emotion, lays down her lyre. At her feet, Oswald and his friends, overwhelmed, are listening to her in a state of ecstasy mixed with anguish, under a stormy sky. In the distance, Vesuvius smoulders. The painter, who was somewhat reluctant to lend Madame de Staël's features to Corinne, treats her in an idealised way; the face of her lover, Oswald, on the other hand, is based directly on that of Prince Augustus himself. The work is a demonstration of the latter's passion for Madame Récamier, to whom he gave it in 1821. It was exhibited in the 1822 Salon.
The highly romantic inspiration of this canvas represents a formal classicism which is very much in the Davidian vein, and the work had a great deal of success. It was hung in Madame Récamier's dining room in L'Abbaye aux Bois, where Chateaubriand read his *Mémoires d'Outre-Tombe*.
D.B.

Théodore Géricault
Rouen, 1791 - Paris, 1824

The Monomaniac of Envy
c. 1819-1822
Oil on canvas
0.72 x 0.58
Acquired in 1908
Inv. B 825

This painting is one of a set of ten portraits of lunatics, only five of which are extant (the other four being in Paris, Ghent, Winterthur and Springfield, Mass.). They were painted by Géricault at the end of his life, no doubt on his return from England in 1821. They were given by the painter to his friend Dr Georget, the head of the psychiatric department in the Salpêtrière hospital, who had published a thesis *On Madness*. This set, which had for long been held in low esteem by Géricault specialists, is now seen as counting among his masterpieces. This particular portrait is astonishing in its realism and psychological penetration; it is one of the most striking that has come down to us from the 19th century, and reveals the depth of Géricault's compassion for human beings ravaged by physical and mental suffering.
D.B.

Georges Michel
Paris, 1763 - 1843

Stormy Landscape
Oil on paper mounted on canvas
0.52 x 0.67
Gift of Mr and Mrs Jean
Charpentier, 1939
Inv. 1939-6

Georges Michel was a solitary artist, and very little is known of his career. He left numerous views of the Seine valley, whose changing landscapes he captured admirably; but few are of a more violently romantic character than this one, which makes one wonder if the painter did not deliberately leave it in the state of a sketch. The storm which is breaking out above the landscape, from which humanity seems to be absent, is a veritable cosmic battle between shade and light, conveyed with a gesturality of astonishing modernity. Going beyond the influence of the Dutch landscape painters, whose works he copied (and also restored, at the Louvre), Michel, in this masterpiece, comes closer to J.M.W. Turner, whose formal audacity he shared.
C.B.

Eugène Delacroix
Charenton-Saint-Maurice, 1798
Paris, 1863

Woman Stroking a Parrot
1827
Oil on canvas
0.245 x 0.325
Gift of Mr Couturier de Royas, 1897
Inv. B 566

This masterpiece, which is contemporary with *The Death of Sardanapalus*, was part of the exhibition that the Colbert gallery put on to aid cholera victims in 1832. For a long time it went unremarked by the public and the critics, before being recognised as one of the jewels of the Musée de Lyon's collection, which also contains the preparatory drawing. Mlle Laure, who posed for this odalisque, was probably also the model for the naked woman lying on Sardanapalus's bed, as well as for *Greece Expiring on the Ruins of Missolonghi*. A great stylistic affinity links this work to the *Study of a Female Nude, Lying on a Divan* (Louvre), dated between 1827 and 1832.
D.B.

Victor Orsel

Oullins, 1795 - Paris, 1850

Good and Evil
1832
Oil on canvas
3.07 x 2.05
Loaned by the State, 1885
Inv. B 376

It was during his stay in Italy, starting in 1829, that Orsel planned this work, which he executed in part before his return to France. He presented it at the 1833 Salon. His contact with the Nazarenes — a group of German religious painters who had come together under the influence of Overbeck and Cornelius in Rome — led him to orientate his aspiration towards a Christian art of a didactic and moralising character, inspired on the formal level by the painters of the quattrocento. *Good and Evil* may be considered as a veritable æsthetic and moral manifesto. The composition develops a Manichean opposition between the stories of two young girls who personify the two principles which have divided up the world between them: one, with her austere virtue, is going towards happiness and redemption, while the other is being led to physical and moral downfall by her dissolute life. The archaic character of the work is reinforced by the unfolding of a cycle of small paintings on a gold background; these develop the narrative, which is punctuated by Latin formulae around the central figures.

D.B.

Hippolyte Flandrin
Lyon, 1809 - Rome, 1864

*Dante, Led by Virgil, Offers
Consolation to the Souls of
the Covetous*
1835
Oil on canvas
2.95 x 2.45
Loaned by the State, 1837
Inv. A 21

Flandrin painted this work — one of his largest easel paintings — while in Rome, as a resident artist at the Académie de France. The scene represented is drawn from Dante's *Divine Comedy*. In Canto III of *Purgatory*, Dante, accompanied by his guide, the poet Virgil, arrives at the second circle, which is concerned with the vice of covetousness. Here he converses with the Souls of the Covetous, who are blind in body and spirit. The theme of blindness, which appears in other works by Flandrin dating from the same period, may be a reference to the grave eye problems from which the artist suffered in 1834. The details of the landscape are faithfully inspired by the poem: there is the arid, desolate mountain, the rocky cliff, the circular road on a narrow cornice without a parapet, for the execution of which Flandrin may have called on his brother Paul, a talented landscape painter. The legibility of the composition, which marks the influence of his master Ingres, is enhanced by the clear distribution of the colours: the "martyrs covered in grey mantles which present the sad colouring of stone" stand in opposition to the sustained tones of Dante's drapings.
Unlike a number of his confreres, who were also fascinated by Dante's poem, Flandrin did not attempt to convey the terror attached to the *Inferno*, preferring the theme of compassion for others, with Dante, leaning slightly towards the unfortunate souls, as its serene, monumental incarnation.
C.B.

Simon Saint-Jean
Lyon, 1808 - Ecully, 1860

The Gardener
1837
Oil on canvas
1.60 x 1.18
Loaned by the State, 1838
Inv. A 24

This painting, was presented at the Salon of 1838, on which occasion it was acquired by the state. It manifests the ambitions of Saint-Jean, who at the time was a young painter of flowers and a former student of Thierriat and Lepage at the École des Beaux-Arts in Lyon. The representation of a graceful young girl in front of a conventional landscape expresses Saint-Jean's desire to renew the flower-painting genre. This figure allowed him to divide up over two levels the bouquets which irresistibly attract one's attention with their profusion of botanical species and the richness of their arrangements. Set off by a discreet ray of sunshine, cultivated and wild flowers are combined in a harmonious totality featuring hollyhocks, dahlias, tulips, bindweed, peonies, and even acanthus leaves (in a discreet allusion to the legend of the invention of the Corinthian capital, as reported by Vitruvius). The style borrows from the tradition of the Dutch school, of which the former "Salon de la Fleur" in the Museum of Fine Arts contained several examples.
C.B.

Louis Janmot
Lyon, 1814 - 1892

Wildflower
1845
Oil on wood
1.03 x 0.83
Acquired in 1893
Inv. B 502

"This simple figure, serious and melancholy, with its fine drawing and slightly raw colours which recall the old German masters [...]. Beyond the fact that the model is very beautiful, well chosen and arranged, there is, in the colour itself and the combination of the greens, pinks and reds, which is a little painful to the eye, a certain mysticity, which is in keeping with the rest — there is a natural harmony between the colour and the drawing": such was the tribute paid by Baudelaire to this work, one of Janmot's masterpieces, when it was exhibited in the Salon of 1845.
D.B.

Nicolas-Toussaint Charlet
Paris, 1792 - 1845

Episode in the Retreat from Russia
1836
Oil on canvas
1.95 x 2.95
Loaned by the State
Inv. A 19

Charlet is best known for his lithographs, which were executed after the fashion of Géricault; he also did a lot for the propagation of the Napoleonic legend. He was a student of Gros (though much less prolific), and it was in the Salon of 1836 that he exhibited this work, which remains his masterpiece, and is indeed one of the most powerful images of the disaster of Napoleon's retreat from Russia. It did not fail to awaken the admiration of Delacroix: "The conception of this work is truly frightening, and the heart constricts before this immense solitude, which is punctuated, here and there, by human forms buried in the snow, sinister markers in this desolate form". Closer to our own time, the great historian of art Henri Focillon has observed that "the breadth of feeling, the boldness of the execution, the beauty of the severe harmony of tones, which are more or less reduced to black and white, yet fresh and rich, are the signs of a master of the first rank." It was no doubt this painting that inspired the famous beginning of Victor Hugo's *Expiation*, in his *Punishments* (1852).
C.B.

Auguste Ravier
Lyon, 1814 - Morestel (Isère), 1895

The Two Parasol Pines
c. 1842-1846
Oil on canvas
0.25 x 0.35
Acquired in 1959
Inv. 1959-25

In 1840, the year after his decisive encounter with Corot in Auvergne, Ravier went to Rome. *The Two Parasol Pines*, which dates from the end of his Italian period (between 1842 and 1846) marked a turning point in the development of his style, which at this point was directly related to Corot's classic Italianate manner of the 1840s. It is true that Ravier's style, as a painter of the landscapes of Crémieu and Morestel, changed subsequently, under the influence of, among other things, Turner's water-colours, moving towards a more audacious technique, which sometimes bordered on abstraction. With his unending variations on the effects of fog and the setting sun on ponds and marshes, Ravier's sole quest was for "pure light".

D.B.

Jules Ziégler
Langres, 1804 - Paris, 1856

*Judith at the Gates
of Bethulia*
1847
Oil on canvas
1.355 x 1.190
Loaned by the State, 1852
Inv. A 2858

Ziégler's *Judith*, which was presented at the Salon of 1847, where it was in competition with a painting by Horace Vernet on the same subject, refers to a passage in the *Book of Judith:* "Then Judith cried out: Praise God! Praise God! And, drawing the head from the sack, she showed it to them, and said: Here is the head of Holofernes, the captain of the Assyrian army." The impression of strength and brutality derives from the frontality of the young murderess, whose half-length representation occupies the entire space of the painting. Her victorious air, full of pride, with her almost-disturbing feline eye, makes her a perfect incarnation of the "femme fatale", dear to the hearts of the romantic writers. Certain details of the clothing indicate Ziégler's desire to set his heroine in a powerfully evocative orientalism. A student of Ingres and Heim, the artist shows himself in this case to be sensitive, above all, to the influence of Italian and Spanish Caravaggism.
C.B.

Eugène Delacroix
Charenton-Saint-Maurice, 1798
Paris, 1863

*The Last Words of the
Emperor Marcus Aurelius*
1844
Oil on canvas
2.60 x 3.48
Loaned by the State, 1860
Inv. A 2928

This painting was exhibited in the Salon of 1845, accompanied by the following text: "Commodus's perverse inclinations had already become manifest: in his dying voice, the emperor commended his son's youth to some friends, who, like himself, were philosophers and Stoics; but their bleak expressions reveal only too clearly the vanity of his wishes, and their own baneful presentiments concerning the future of the Roman empire". The personage of the emperor-philosopher was particularly dear to Delacroix, who had thought that this subject might be suitable for the library of the Palais Bourbon, the seat of parliament. Drawing his inspiration from the ancient world, the "source of everything", he took up once more, following David (*The Death of Socrates*), the great tradition of French historical painting that had begun with Poussin (*The Death of Germanicus*). This work (which at first seems not to have completely satisfied the artist) was somewhat coolly received by the critics, with the exception of Baudelaire, who was much taken by it, and who called it "a splendid painting, magnificent, sublime, misunderstood [...]. The colour [...] far from losing its cruel originality in this new, more complete scene, is still bloody and terrible". The sketch which Delacroix did for his student Louis de Planet, to serve as a guide for the transfer of the work onto canvas, is also in the Musée de Lyon's collection.

D.B.

Théodore Chassériau
Sainte-Barbe-de-Samana (Saint-Domingue), 1819 - Paris, 1856

The Defence of the Gauls
Paper mounted on canvas
1.167 x 0.905
Gift of Baron Arthur Chassériau,
1926
Inv. B 1379

This is the second complete sketch for a painting which is to be found in the Musée Bargoin in Clermont Ferrand, and which the artist sent to the World Fair of 1855. This work disconcerted Chassériau's contemporaries. The critics, on the whole, were severe, and talked about "exuberant, itinerant decadence", and a "shamelessness of the palette", which they imputed to the excessive, and harmful, influence of Delacroix over Chassériau, who was a student of Ingres. Nonetheless the painter, in this case, was most faithful to the text of Cæsar's *Commentaries* (Book VII) from which he drew his inspiration: "Commanded by Vercingetorix, the Gauls drove back Cæsar's legions from Gergovia. Their dishevelled women implored them, holding up their children on the ramparts and urging them on to combat." This powerful study, painted in brown tones, establishes, in spite of certain later changes, the definitive placing of the main figures involved.
D.B.

Antoine-Louis Barye
Paris, 1795 - 1875

Tiger Devouring a Young Stag
1835
Stone
H. 0.62; L. 1.05; Depth 0.67
Loaned by the State, 1836
Inv. H 792

After creating a sensation with his *Tiger Devouring a Gavial* in the Salon of 1831, and his *Lion and Serpent* in 1833 (both in the Louvre), Barye exhibited a bronze *Tiger Devouring a Young Stag* in 1835. The piece in the Musée de Lyon, which was the first animal group sculpted in stone by this artist, presumably figured in the Salon of 1836, at which time the state acquired it for the Museum of Fine Arts. Barye was fascinated by the savagery of nature, and transposed into the animal domain the romantic æsthetic that his master Gros had passed on to him. The direct observation of "living models" in the menagerie of the Jardin des Plantes, which he visited frequently in the company of Delacroix, gives an astonishing realism to his animal combats, while the extreme precision with which the fur is portrayed recalls his training as an engraver. The edge of the plinth is curiously ornamented with a frieze of aquatic animals (crocodiles, fish, etc.).
C.B.

Jean-Baptiste Carpeaux
Valenciennes, 1827
Courbevoie, 1875

La Palombella
1861
Plaster
H. 0.45; L. 0.28; Depth 0.29
Acquired in 1963
Inv. 1963-9

During his residence at the Villa Medicis, Carpeaux fell in love with a young peasant girl, Barbera Pasquarelli ("la Palombella"), who was born in 1842 in Palombarra, a village near Rome. This idyll was cut short by her death at the age of nineteen, but her memory remained for a long time a source of inspiration to the sculptor. He represented her, firstly, in the antique manner, then in a regional hat, called "pane", then with a necklace and a chignon of curls, crowned with flowers and ears of corn, as a representation of "summer", and finally as an allegory of "the Republic". This first bust, of which there are two other plaster versions (now in the Musée du Petit Palais, Paris, and the Villa Medicis, Rome), is marked by the extreme simplicity of the pose, bringing out the purity of the lines of the face, which is characterised by a sense of gravity. Besides the very accomplished technique, this piece is interesting for the dedication, dated Rome, 1861, to his friend, the painter Félix-Auguste Clément (1826-1888), who was a fellow resident at the Villa Medicis.
C.B.

Louis Janmot
Lyon, 1814 - 1892

The Poem of the Soul:
The Wrong Path
1854
Oil on canvas
1.10 x 1.42
Gift of the artist's family, 1968
Inv. 1968-163

Janmot began *The Poem of the Soul* in 1847. The cycle was to comprise thirty-four paintings, but in fact only eighteen were executed and exhibited (in 1854 and 1855). For the sixteen other compositions, Janmot did no more than the sketches (which are also in the Museum of Fine Arts). In 1881 he published a poem of four thousand lines, as a commentary upon this mystical story of a soul.

The Poem of the Soul is incontestably the masterpiece of the mystical current that blossomed in Lyonnais painting around 1840 as an expression of the movement of Catholic renewal, and which was closely linked to Pre-Raphaelism. Baudelaire's judgement of the work was mixed: "This story of a soul is turbid and confused [...] Monsieur Janmot does not have a philosophically sound brain [but] it has to be recognised that from the point of view of pure art there is in the composition of these scenes, and even in the bitter colours which they have been given, a charm which is infinite and difficult to describe: something of the sweetness of solitude, of the sacristy, the church, the cloister; an unconscious, childlike mysticity."

The Wrong Path, which was the seventh composition in the cycle, represents a moment when the two young heroes of the *Poem*, who are about to enter the university, are confronted with the dangers of false science, which lies in wait for them in the form of professors in rows of niches, who threaten to destroy their faith. The critics were rightly happier about the fantastic character of the composition than the topical polemical allusions to the struggle against the state's monopolistic control over the universities.
D.B.

Pierre Puvis de Chavannes
Lyon, 1824 - Paris, 1898

Autumn
1864
Oil on canvas
2.85 x 2.26
Loaned by the State, 1864
Inv. A 2963

This work represents a continuation of those that decorate the museum of Amiens (dated between 1861 and 1864). And it may be that Puvis, when painting this large decorative canvas — whose theme, which was then much in vogue, often provided him with inspiration — thought about executing a set of four panels for Amiens, on the theme of the seasons. The critics gave the work a mixed reception at the Salon of 1864. Castagnary, for example, did not like its hermetic character: "this stylish painting, which is meant to uplift the soul while it charms the eyes! [...] A brochure no longer suffices: M. Puvis de Chavannes's *Autumn* needs ten pages of description!"

No doubt the figure of the seated woman wearing a blue dress (a colour which Puvis often used for his elderly figures) symbolises maturity, the autumn of life. She is contemplating with serene detachment the insouciant nudity of two young women seen in a standing position.

D.B.

Hippolyte Flandrin
Lyon, 1809 - Rome, 1864

Self-portrait
c. 1860
Oil on canvas
0.67 x 0.54
Bequest by the son of the artist,
Hippolyte Flandrin, 1928
Inv. B 1555

If we may take for granted the commonly accepted dating of this work, i.e. around 1860, Flandrin's features, as they are presented to us here, are prematurely aged, given that he was only around fifty at the time. Adopting the traditional pose of the artist before a mirror, he portrays himself at his easel, brush in hand. His face is half in shadow, in an attempt to conceal his squint, which had become more accentuated with time. The painting recommends itself to us by the fine quality of its light and chiaroscuro, which express with sensitivity the artist's melancholy.
C.B.

Jean-François Millet
Gruchy (Gréville, Manche), 1814 - Barbizon, 1875

A Naval Officer
1845
Oil on canvas
0.81 x 0.65
Acquired in 1905
Inv. B 759

In 1845 Millet, who had just lost his young wife, Pauline Ono, went to live for three months in Le Havre, where he painted more than a dozen portraits of the painters and personalities of the port, as a way of making some money. This particular portrait of an officer, along with one which is now in the Musée des Beaux-Arts in Rouen, dates from this period, shortly after which he returned to Paris. The model, who is wearing a lieutenant's uniform, is seen in profile, his head turned towards the spectator, his sword under his arm, in a less conventional pose than that of his Rouen counterpart. He is seen against an evening sky crossed by clouds, and this adds to the melancholy character of his expression, which Millet has conveyed with admirable psychological acuity.
C.B.

Jean-Baptiste Camille Corot
Paris, 1796 - 1875

The Studio
1870
Oil on canvas
0.63 x 0.48
Acquired in 1901
Inv. B 627

Starting in 1865, Corot painted several variations on the theme of the model seated in front of an easel in a studio. This particular work, which is the only one to be dated, is among the most profoundly moving of the series. The mandolin which accompanies the other figures has been replaced, in this case, by a half-open book on the young woman's knees, and this is perhaps the source of the reverie which has diverted her attention from the contemplation of the painting placed before her. She is wearing a light-coloured veil, and her face, with its large melancholy eyes, is seen in three-quarters profile. Illuminated by the declining daylight through the glass roof, she is seen against the wall of the studio, near a small still-life representation (which constitutes an exception in Corot's work) of red flowers in a vase and a lemon on a plate. This painting, which is one of the artist's masterpieces, is marked by discreet pathos; this may be explained by the bereavements which clouded the artist's life in 1870.
C.B.

Gustave Courbet

Ornans, 1819 - La Tour de Peilz
(Switzerland), 1877

The Wave

Oil on canvas

0.66 x 0.90

Acquired in 1881

Inv. B 295

"Do not look for something symbolic, as in the style of Cabanel or Baudry — some nude woman or other, her flesh pearly as a conch, bathing in an agate sea. Courbet has quite simply painted a wave, a real wave breaking on the shore". Thus it was that Zola presented *The Wave*, which Courbet exhibited in the 1870 Salon. Among the numerous versions of this seascape, the example shown here is perhaps one of the most striking; it is similar to those which are to be found in Bremen and Berlin. The same billows of the raging sea seem to respond to the threatening unruliness of the sky, which for the artist is first and foremost a pretext for an extraordinary piece of painting. The work was painted on the Normandy coast, where Courbet met Boudin and Monet; the robustness of its technique, and its author's attachment to muted tones, are what distance it from the Impressionists' researches.

C.B.

Honoré Daumier

Marseille, 1808 - Valmondois, 1879

Passers-by

Oil on canvas

0.59 x 1.15

Acquired in 1904

Inv. B 684

Among the three versions of the theme of passers-by in Daumier's work, this one, which is undated (like all the artist's works), is the most accomplished. Here, he uses a horizontal format, which allows him to unfold his composition like a frieze, with an anonymous crowd hurrying along a Parisian pavement before a façade that is barely suggested. The few faces that are turned towards the spectator are powerfully modelled by the light, looming out from a rich camaïeu of browns. These closed, almost disquieting faces are not unrelated to the figures that Daumier caricatured in innumerable lithographs. The spontaneity of the technique, reinforced by the fact that the painting is unfinished (as is often the case in Daumier's work), transfigures the banality of this street scene, into which the artist's genius has infused the character of a Goyaesque vision.

C.B.

Louis Carrand
Lyon, 1821 - 1899

The Cours du Midi, Lyon
c. 1860
Oil on paper mounted on canvas
0.235 x 0.320
Acquired in 1912
Inv. B 991

Like his friend Ravier, Louis Carrand was essentially a landscape artist. He was a solitary painter, who walked throughout the Monts du Lyonnais countryside, where he produced numerous studies. He was intrigued by the optical theories of the chemist Chevreul, and worked at expressing the ceaselessly changing effects of light, using juxtaposed pale-coloured, silvery touches. At the beginning of his career, Carrand was close to the Barbizon school; subsequently, landscapes like this one, which can be dated to the 1860s, made him a precursor of the Impressionists, though in fact he had no real personal contact with them. This urban view, which prefigures certain of Pissarro's Parisian views, takes for its subject a street (now the Cours de Verdun) which runs between the Rhône and the Saône in the Perrache district. This street has been greatly changed in recent times by the transformations carried out on the peninsula between the two rivers. This autumnal landscape is enlivened by small, expressive silhouettes of passers-by coming and going, cuirassiers on horseback, and a carriage circling in the foreground.
C.B.

Adolphe Monticelli
Marseille, 1824 - 1886

Bridge over the Huveaune
c. 1871-1872
Oil on canvas
0.69 x 0.93
Léon and Louise Charbonnier
Bequest, 1951
Inv. 1951-69

This canvas shows a river near Marseille. Monticelli was much taken by the powerful architecture of the bridge, which is the centrepiece of his composition, whose frankness and monumentality recall the landscapes of Courbet, with whom Monticelli, as a Provençal, shared a taste for layers of colour whose uniform distribution over the entire surface of the painting, in this instance, sets up a veritable visual continuum. This profoundly original style conveys a feeling for nature that is comparable to the landscapes of Diaz de la Peña, a painter of the Barbizon school who was his mentor.

Monticelli is remarkably well represented in the Museum of Fine Arts thanks to the Charbonnier Bequest, which in 1951 brought the museum around thirty paintings.

C.B.

Pascal-Adolphe-Jean
Dagnan-Bouveret
Paris, 1852 - Quincy (Haute Saône),
1929

A Wedding Party
at the Photographer's Studio
1879
Oil on canvas
0.85 x 1.22
Gift of Jacques Bernard, 1879
Inv. H 715

Dagnan-Bouveret, who was a student of Gérôme and Cabanel, presented this painting, which was begun in 1878, at the 1879 Salon, where it was very popular with the critics and the public. It is a genre scene, and is linked to the circumstances of the painter's own marriage. "I am very fond of this subject — it gives me infinite pleasure to execute, and moreover it speaks to me, as it were, of you each day", he wrote to Maria Walter, whom he later married. The entire scene is painstakingly described, with a taste for anecdote and a sense of detail that appears to be trying to vie with the possibilities offered by the camera, which is the real subject of the painting. It is a highly symbolic fact about this dialogue between painting and photography that Dagnan-Bouveret, as a way of thanking the photographer for allowing him to do a small painted study of the latter's studio, commissioned him to do his portrait. During a visit to the Museum of Fine Arts thirty years later, seeing this "youthful error", Dagnan exclaimed, in a letter to his wife: "What a punishment, to have made such a mistake! But perhaps it is true that without some such impulse I would never have recognised the limits of my art, nor have rediscovered my path afterwards."
C.B.

Ernest Meissonier
Lyon, 1815 - Poissy, 1891

General Championnet
beside the Sea
1882
Oil on wood
0.225 x 0.360
Acquired in 1893
Inv. B 509

Abandoning the extreme precision which characterised most of his works, whether historical subjects or genre scenes inspired by the minor Dutch masters of the 17th century, Meissonier nonetheless succeeded in imprinting an epic spirit upon this small work. The main personage is General Jean-Étienne Championnet (1762-1800), who, after his break with Napoleon following the latter's *coup d'État,* retired to Antibes. No particular anecdote is illustrated in this scene, which has all the liberty and spirited nature of a fleeting vision, unless one chooses to see the struggle of the figures against the hostile elements as a metaphor of Championnet's republican opposition to the rising tide of Napoleon's ambitions. Meissonier was familiar with the beach where the scene is set; it features in several of his landscape studies, and also in the 1868 *Outing on Horseback* (Musée d'Orsay), in which he included a portrait of himself.
C.B.

Alfred Sisley
Paris, 1839 - Moret sur Loing, 1899

The Seine at Marly
1876
Oil on canvas
0.60 x 0.74
Acquired in 1903
Inv. B 660

At Marly le Roi, where he lived from 1875 to 1878 in a small house in Avenue de l'Abreuvoir, Sisley produced a score of paintings based on the landscapes he found around him. The admirably structured composition of the one shown here gives its full importance to the theme of the bend in the road, of which Sisley was so fond, on account of the way it allowed him to deepen space. The large trees in the foreground hint at the concern with monumentality felt by this "painter of river banks", whose essential interest was the study of atmospheric values, the quality of light and the way it glinted on water. This painting was done at the same time as the *Flood at Port Marly* (Musée d'Orsay), which gave Sisley the inspiration for a series of compositions.
C.B.

Henri Fantin-Latour
Grenoble, 1836 - Buré (Orne), 1904

The Reading
1877
Oil on canvas
0.97 x 1.30
Acquired in 1901
Inv. B 628

Among the numerous portraits of members of his family circle, Fantin-Latour executed four compositions featuring two female figures: *The Two Sisters*, 1859 (Saint Louis), another *Reading*, 1870 (Lisbon), painted before the *Reading* shown here, and *The Drawing Lesson*, 1879 (Brussels). In these works, which the painter did not consider as genre scenes, but as portraits, the two women, even when they are linked by a common activity, remain totally removed from each other; it is always a question of the juxtaposition of two solitudes. Fantin-Latour's sister-in-law, Charlotte Dubourg, who is so often present in his works, and whose silhouette stands out here in a pure profile, does not seem to be concerned by the reading which absorbs her companion. The reference to the silent, immobile interior scenes of the 17th century Dutch painters is a constant in Fantin-Latour's group portraits.
D.B.

Edgar Degas (Hilaire Germain Edgar de Gas, called)
Paris, 1834 - 1917

The Café-Concert at "Les Ambassadeurs"
1876-1877
Pastel on monotype
0.37 x 0.26
Acquired in 1910
Inv. B 917

The "café-concerts" in the gardens of the Champs-Élysées, of which the one at "Les Ambassadeurs" was among the best known, began in the 1830s, and reached their apogee towards 1870. The singers who performed there, like Mlle Bécat, shown here, whom Degas portrayed several times, fascinated him by their gestural excessiveness, as well as the vivacity, at once witty, vulgar and provocative, with which they interpreted their songs before a largely working-class public. This series of monotypes can in all probability be dated to the years 1876-1877.

The monotype was a new process, which Degas used frequently, though he preferred to speak of "drawings done in oil-based ink, then printed". The technique consisting of drawing on a plate entirely covered with ink, proceeding by the removal of the latter so that the drawing showed up clearly on a dark background. Furthermore, Degas often used pastel to retouch his monotypes. The process provided Degas with new resources in his research into the effects of artificial lighting. In this work, the row of Japanese lanterns whose reflections can be seen in the mirror framed by the two fluted columns amplifies, with its diagonal form, the gesture of the singer, and prolongs it indefinitely.

In the third Impressionist exhibition in April 1877, Degas exhibited a set of monotypes highlighted with pastel, including two scenes set in Les Ambassadeurs (the other of which is in the Corcoran Gallery of Art in Washington).

D.B.

Edouard Manet
Paris, 1832 - 1883

Marguerite Gauthier-Lathuille
Oil on canvas
0.51 x 0.50
Acquired in 1902
Inv. B 643

The "Père Lathuille" was a famous restaurant beside the Café Guerbois where "the Manet gang" met, and which the artist immortalised in 1879 in his famous painting *At Père Lathuille's* (Musée de Tournai). The owner's daughter always denied having posed for this portrait, which was painted, it would seem, from rapid sketches executed unbeknown to the young girl. Here Manet's art reaches a high degree of refinement, both in the nuances of the deliberately restricted range of colours, the extreme economy of means, and the lightness and transparence of the technique.
D.B.

Claude Monet

Paris, 1840 - Giverny, 1926

Rough Sea at Étretat

1883

Oil on canvas

0.81 x 1.00

Acquired in 1902

Inv. B 647

Étretat was often visited by the painters of the 19th century, but Monet, who painted it often, is perhaps the artist with whom it is most generally associated. During the winter of 1883, he stayed there for about three weeks. As a result of persistent bad weather, he was forced to work under cover in "an annex of the hotel [the Blanquet], from which one has a superb view of the cliff and the boats". From this spot, where he painted four canvases, Monet saw the cliff and the Porte d'Aval from close up, and had a view over the shore where the boats were beached. Three old boats covered with thatch, which the fishermen used for storing their gear, occupy the foreground of this painting. The effect of vibration produced by the natural stratification of the cliff provides an echo to the agitation of the waves.

D.B.

Vincent Van Gogh
Groot Zundert (Netherlands), 1853 -
Auvers sur Oise, 1890

*Peasant Woman with
a Green Shawl*
1885
Oil on canvas
0.45 x 0.35
Acquired in 1937
Inv. 1937-34

This work belongs to a set of studies of heads done by Van Gogh at Nuenen between December 1884 and the end of April 1885. The same woman, seen almost face-on, appears in another of these studies, which is now in the Van Gogh museum in Amsterdam; and it is presumably one of these two works that is referred to by the artist in a letter to his brother Theo, dated 1 June 1885. This particular work would seem to have been inspired by Zola's description, in *Germinal*, of a woman about to be hanged. It is contemporaneous with the famous *Potato Eaters*, and is characteristic of the sombre manner that marked the artist's Dutch period, before he moved to Paris. He was trying at that time to express the tragic condition of the common people, peasants and weavers, with whose physical poverty and moral isolation he identified so closely. Before its inclusion in the museum's collection, the work belonged to the painter Henri Le Fauconnier (1881-1946).
C.B.

Paul Gauguin
Paris, 1848 - Atuana, Hiva Oa
(Marquesas Islands), 1903

Nave Nave Mahana
1896
Oil on canvas
0.95 x 1.30
Acquired in 1913
Inv. B 1038

This major work, the most important of Gauguin's to be found in a French public collection, dates from the painter's second stay in Tahiti. In 1895, after spending two years in Paris, Gauguin went back to settle permanently in Oceania, first in Tahiti and then in the Marquesas Islands, where he died in 1903. This period, though marked by illness and despair, was particularly productive: in 1896 and 1897, he sent two consignments of canvases to France, including the work shown here, whose Maori name means "delightful days". The audacity and sumptuousness of the extraordinary colours, the nobility of the figures and the composition, with the skilful cadence of its solemn hieraticism, are the essential characteristics of this canvas, which was part of Henri Rouart's collection, sold in 1912.
D.B.

Pierre-Auguste Renoir
Limoges, 1841
Cagnes-sur-Mer, 1919

Woman Playing the Guitar
1897
Oil on canvas
0.81 x 0.65
Acquired in 1901
Inv. B 624

At the end of the 1890s Renoir executed a series of paintings representing men and women playing the guitar. This particular work, which is without doubt among the finest of them, is probably the one which Julie Manet admired in the painter's studio in February 1897: "He does delightful things with the guitar: a woman in a white muslin dress with pink ribbons is bending gracefully over the large yellow guitar, one foot resting on a yellow cushion... Everything is coloured, soft, delicious." At that time Renoir's art was evolving towards a certain monumental classicism; he was abandoning modern dress and giving his figures fantasy costumes, adopting a more atemporal or exotic style, as in the Spanish-style dress of the guitarist in this painting. In their inspiration, these compositions recall the female figures painted by Corot, which Renoir admired particularly.

D.B.

Paul Cézanne
Aix-en-Provence, 1839 - 1906

Bathers
c. 1890-1900
Oil on canvas
0.22 x 0.33
Loaned by the State, 1986
Inv. 1986-201

The theme of the bather — male or female — is, with that of the Montagne Sainte Victoire, one of those that Cézanne came back to continually up until the end of his life. From 1870 onwards, there was a succession of variations on this subject, of which *The Large Bathers* in Philadelphia is the culmination. Through the study of the nude in a landscape, these compositions, which occupy the frontier between the mythological theme and the memory of real experience, tirelessly pursue the project of research on the integration of volumes into space.

D.B.

Édouard Vuillard
Cuiseaux (Saône-et-Loire), 1868
La Baule, 1940

*Misia at Villeneuve
sur Yonne*
1897-1899
Oil on plywood
0.42 x 0.62
Gift of Mrs Bremont and Mrs Lignel,
1967
Inv. 1967-4

In the spring of 1897, Misia and Thadée Natanson bought "Le Relais", a beautiful house at Villeneuve, on the banks of the Yonne, where they entertained their numerous friends. It was then that Vuillard executed this interior, where he portrayed Misia, of whom he was a fervent admirer; she was at the centre of the gatherings which brought together the artists of *La Revue blanche*, edited by Thadée, and often sat for the Nabi painters. It was this same theme of figures in interiors, which is treated here with extreme refinement in simplicity, that inspired Vuillard's great decorative masterpieces.
D.B.

Medardo Rosso
Turin, 1858 - Milan, 1928

Impression of a Boulevard.
Woman with a Veil
Wax on plaster
H. 0.75; L. 0.65; Depth 0.29
Loaned by the State, 1931
Inv. H 822

The *Woman with a Veil* is the most important of Rosso's sculptures to be found in France, though it was in fact in France that, after his naturalisation in 1902, he produced the major part of his work. He was a powerfully original sculptor, who pushed to the limits his research into the notion of "Impressionist sculpture", which had a certain influence on Rodin's *Balzac*: "The sculptor must, by a summary of received impressions, communicate everything that has affected his own sensitivity, so that when one looks at his work one will experience entirely the emotion he himself felt when observing nature", he declared in 1902. Modelled wax on a wooden armature appeared to him, in its ductility and the effects of translucence that it made possible, as the most suitable medium for conveying the fleeting impression of a passer-by whose memory the artist could not separate out from the space around her. Clémenceau, who was Prime Minister at that time, was enthusiastic about the work, which he picked out in Rosso's studio in 1907; he had it bought for the Musée du Luxembourg. It was misunderstood, and was never exhibited, nor even recorded in the museum's inventory. It was sent to Lyon after the removal of the state's collection of works in marble, among which it had remained forgotten.
C.B.

Odilon Redon
Bordeaux, 1840 - Paris, 1916

Half-length Figure
Pastel
0.45 x 0.32
Acquired in 1911
Inv. B 965

Towards 1890 Redon began to abandon charcoal in favour of pastels and paint, with the "Blacks" making way for light and colour. This figure, which is not dissimilar to that of a Christ suffering, can be situated among those to which the imagination of the great precursor of the Symbolists gave a spiritual life of such intensity and individuality. It was the "closed eyes" motif seen here — as so frequently in Redon's work — that gave its title to a celebrated painting which is to be found in the Louvre.
D.B.

Alexandre Séon
Chazelles-sur-Lyon, 1855
Paris, 1917

Sâr Joséphin Péladan
1892
Oil on canvas
1.32 x 0.80
Gift of the artist's widow, 1936
Inv. 1936-50

Alexandre Séon, a student and collaborator of Puvis de Chavannes, was one of the founders, along with Péladan and Count de la Rochefoucauld, of a Rosicrucian group that was involved in the spiritual renewal of the arts. It was at the first Salon of the Order in 1892 that Séon exhibited this portrait of the author of *The Supreme Vice*. It was probably Léon Bloy who persuaded Péladan that he was an Assyrian, and that he was a descendant of Baladan Merodack, the king of Babylon, of whose name his own was a Western derivation. Péladan much appreciated Séon's portrait of him: "You have painted the Sâr, and not only have you painted him with the comprehension of the Chaldean features that characterise him, but you have painted the soul of the Sâr!... This marvellous work explains the word Sâr in its true sense, as a priest of the idea, knight of the Grail and envoy of Montsalvat." In effect, the work fully lived up to Rosicrucian æsthetic requirements for the art of the portrait: the point was to "attain the style", and not to "date the costume". The "Chaldean" costume, the hieratic medal-profile, the dominance of the line, the attenuation of the volumes — everything contributes to the spiritualisation of this figure, which Camille Mauclair described as a "mummified portrait of the Sâr in a mauve robe".
D.B.

Gustave Moreau
Paris, 1836 - 1898

Chaste Susannah
Oil on wood
0.52 x 0.33
Gift of Mr Baillehache, 1923
Inv. B 1297

In this superb work, Gustave Moreau recalls that of his much-respected master, Théodore Chassériau. The mere suggestion of the décor, enveloped in a mysterious shadow, gives its full brilliance to this nude, with its monumental beauty. The theme of "Susannah and the Elders" inspired two other compositions by Moreau (now in private collections), which, however, in the importance given to the décor, and its precision, along with the richness of Susannah's apparel, stand in marked contrast to the simplicity of this particular painting.
D.B.

Pierre Puvis de Chavannes
Lyon, 1824 - Paris, 1898

Princess Marie Cantacuzène
1883
Oil on canvas
0.78 x 0.46
Bequest by the model, 1899
Inv. B 606

Puvis de Chavannes would seem to have met Marie Cantacuzène around 1856 in the studio of her painter friend Chassériau. He told one of his first biographers of the considerable influence exerted over him by this highly cultivated woman, who became his lifetime companion, collaborator and inspiration. She was born in 1820 in Moldavia, into a noble Roumanian family. Around 1850 she left her husband, Prince Alexander Cantacuzène, to come to Paris. She married Puvis in 1897. This portrait, one of the finest examples of "portraits of the century", in Paul Baudoüin's words, was favourably received by the critics at the 1883 Salon. Péladan wrote: "Around him there are only *skilful hands*; he himself is a thought [...] He is such a thinker that, in portraying, he reaches the level of the abstract. Mme C [...] is not a widow, she is *the* widow [...] M. Puvis de Chavannes is the greatest painter of this time, even as a portraitist, since he makes the portrait the very type of a state of being, and the abstraction of a feeling". Puvis was however annoyed by this interpretation, and commented on the work, in a letter dated June 1883, "to warn against the legend that has been constructed around my portrait at the Salon. This person is not a widow, and if her expression is sorrowful, the fault is mine, for having involuntarily accentuated it in that direction. Hers is a serious spirit, highly exalted and benevolent. My only excuse is to have seen her often in this pensive attitude, which may be misleading. Thoughtful people do not think gaily, but in the present case there is no immediate distress."

Princess Cantacuzène often figured in Puvis's work. She lent her features to Salome in *The Beheading of John the Baptist*, to the *Radegonde* that is now in the Town Hall of Poitiers, and to the *Sainte Genevieve* in the Pantheon, among others.

D.B.

Raoul Dufy
Le Havre, 1877 - Forcalquier, 1953

Boat Decked Out with Flags
c. 1905
Oil on canvas
0.54 x 0.65
Anonymous gift, 1927
Inv. B 1457

Dufy was highly impressed by Matisse's *Luxury, Calm and Voluptuousness* (Musée d'Orsay), which he discovered in March 1905 at the Salon d'Automne. At that time he was starting to break free from the influence of Impressionism, and to adopt the Fauvist æsthetic of which this Salon saw the birth. A comparison between his *Yacht Decked Out with Flags*, painted in 1904 (Musée des Beaux-Arts, Le Havre), and this *Boat Decked Out with Flags*, both of whose subjects he had, no doubt, observed in the Bassin du Commerce in Le Havre, demonstrates this development. What is striking in the composition is the directness of the way in which the ship, seen close up, crosses the field of the canvas. The theme of flags, which had been popular since the Impressionists, favoured the blossoming of pure colour, which contrasts here with the white of the hull and the preparatory coating, which the artist has allowed to remain visible. Dufy's style bears a certain relation to that of his friend Albert Marquet, who, in the summer of 1906, joined him in Le Havre, painting numerous landscapes there, as well as in Trouville and Honfleur.
C.B.

Albert Marquet
Bordeaux, 1875 - Paris, 1947

The Port of Hamburg
1909
Oil on canvas
0.81 x 0.60
Mr and Mrs Léon Bouchut Bequest,
1974
Inv. 1974-32

Marquet spent the winter of 1909 in Hamburg, where he painted a series of canvases representing the port. This painting is characteristic of the "dark period" which in 1908 succeeded the highly coloured audaciousness of his Fauvist works; here Marquet uses an austere palette dominated by browns and greys. From this point on, his favourite theme was landscapes of rivers and ports, for which he often, as in this case, adopted a bird's-eye view. The simplified masses are outlined in black, the wide curve of the river burying itself in the canvas under a heavy sky in the immobility of the cold wintry light.
D.B.

Georges Braque
Argenteuil-sur-Seine, 1882
Paris, 1963

Violin
1911
Oil on canvas
0.73 x 0.60
Gift of Raoul La Roche, 1954
Inv. 1955-3

From 1909-1910 onwards, Braque and Picasso worked in close collaboration on their research into the spatial construction of the canvas. Together they elaborated what was known as "Analytical Cubism", which was characterised by the total disintegration of the object, with a more and more intense fragmentation of the surface into a multitude of facets, and greys, ochres and browns covering the entire canvas. Around the same time, Braque gave some of his pieces an oval form which produced a concentrated space. This format allowed him to bring out the significance of his work on the flatness of the support by eliminating the corners of the canvas, those neutral zones which often give the illusion of a receding background, recreating a third dimension that Braque was in fact trying to do away with altogether. The "papiers collés" which were to follow often took on this format. Musical instruments — mandolins, guitars, violins, flutes, clarinets — associated with human figures and other objects constitute one of the leitmotifs of Cubist iconography.
D.B.

Michel Larionov
(Mikhaïl Feodorovich)
Tiraspol, 1881
Fontenay-aux-Roses, 1964

Vladimir Burliuk (1886-1917)
1910
Oil on canvas
1.33 x 1.04
Acquired in 1967
Inv. 1967-245

It was in 1910 that Larionov did this portrait of the painter Vladimir Burliuk, whose career was tragically cut short by the First World War. The two men, along with Burliuk's brother David, Nathalie Gontcharova, Kusnetsov and Yakulov El-Saryan, founded the "Blue Rose" group, whose mouthpiece was a journal called *The Golden Fleece*. This was the period when, liberated from the Impressionist and Pointillist influences that marked the beginning of his career, and drawn to Russian popular art, Larionov produced a series of powerfully original works incorporating a number of lines of research, some of which recall those pursued by the German Expressionists of the time. The radically new character of the canvases which he presented at three successive *Golden Fleece* exhibitions, among which the most famous was the series of *Soldiers*, followed by that of *Hairdressers*, made him the uncontested leader of the Russian avant-garde.
D.B.

Roger de La Fresnaye
Le Mans, 1885 - Grasse, 1925

Alice with a Large Hat
1912
Oil on canvas
1.30 x 0.97
Acquired in 1951
Inv. 1952-21

This portrait of Madame Henri de la Fresnaye, the artist's sister-in-law, was exhibited, along with *The Cuirassier* (on loan to the Museum of Fine Arts from the Musée National d'Art Moderne) and the second version of *The Artillery*, in the Salon des Indépendants in 1912, when the artist was setting out on one of the most productive periods of his career. Here he brilliantly expresses a highly personal conception of Cubism, whose influence he was at that time experiencing. Having joined the Groupe de Puteaux in 1911, he took part in the gatherings in Jacques Villon's studio at the time of the formation of the Section d'Or, a group of artists who sought to systematise the Cubist approach. This splendid portrait, whose preparatory drawing is to be found in the Musée National d'Art Moderne, gives an idea of the talent possessed by this student of Maurice Denis and Sérusier.
C.B.

Suzanne Valadon
Bessines-sur-Gartempe 1867
Paris, 1938

*Marie Coca
and her Daughter*
1913
Oil on canvas
1.61 x 1.30
Acquired from the artist, 1935
Inv. 1935-51

This double portrait of Suzanne Valadon's niece and grand-niece, presented at the Salon des Indépendants in 1913, should be seen in the framework of Valadon's series of large collective portraits of her immediate family. The authority of the line, the force and simplicity of the composition, the deliberately accentuated perspective of the floor (which seems to project the figures forwards), the expressive acuteness of the faces — all of these demonstrate the depth of the painter's technical mastery. The reproduction of a painting by Degas, seen hanging on the wall, is Valadon's tribute to the painter of dancers, who had given her encouragement and urged her to begin exhibiting in the Salon of the Société Nationale des Beaux-Arts in 1882.
D.B.

Léopold Survage
Moscow, 1879 - Paris, 1968

Factories
1914
Oil on canvas
0.81 x 0.65
Acquired in 1968
Inv. 1968-128

In 1908, after studying at the school of fine arts in Moscow, Survage came to live in Paris. As a student of Matisse, to begin with, he was influenced by Cubism, to which he gave a highly personal interpretation. Unlike Braque and Picasso, who were mostly doing still lifes and portraits, he did not hesitate to tackle the space of the landscape, which he broke up into geometrical sequences inherited from the "facets" of Analytical Cubism. Painted at the time when Survage began planning his film *Rythme coloré* (a radical contribution to the history of abstraction), *Factories* is one of the most important works of the period, transcribing an industrial landscape into a montage inspired by cinematographic techniques: the succession of close-up views of brick chimneys, and the rosette on the aeroplane, suggest, in effect, the technique of the tracking shot. This work, in the attention it gives to the disquieting poetry of the modern city, and the anticipation of Surrealist juxtapositions of incongruous elements, was no doubt influenced by the work of de Chirico, whom Apollinaire had brought to Survage's attention at the 1913 Salon d'Automne.

C.B.

Albert Gleizes
Paris, 1881 - Avignon, 1953

Juliette Roche
1915
Oil on canvas
0.615 x 0.365
Gift of Mrs Albert Gleizes, 1954
Inv. 1954-119

This small painting, one of the jewels in the museum's large collection of Albert Gleizes's works, demonstrates the painter's attachment to the human figure and the portrait form. Among his models were friends such as the publisher Eugène Figuière (whose 1913 portrait is owned by the museum), and the musicians Igor Stravinsky (1914) and Florent Schmitt (1915). The work shown here, which is of a more intimate kind, depicts the Paris police chief's daughter, Juliette Roche, whom Gleizes married the following year. This work leans heavily on Cubist doctrines, of which Gleizes, along with Metzinger, was one of the main theorists — they published *On Cubism* in 1912. This painting, with its use of coloured planes and dynamic geometry, prefigures the plastic system developed by the artist during the 1920s.
C.B.

Gino Severini
Cortone, 1883 - Paris, 1966

The Painter's Family
1936
Oil on canvas
1.74 x 1.18
Acquired from the artist, 1939
Inv. 1939-13

In the middle of the 1930s, after having largely contributed to the Futurist avant-garde movement, Severini returned to the monumental portrait and, in a sense, gave Italian portrait painting its definitive character for the century. In the second quadrennial of Rome, in 1935, he exhibited a portrait of his wife, Jeanne (which is now in Budapest), and one of his daughter, Gina (now in Turin). The painting seen here, which was exhibited in Paris in 1937, is highly representative of this series of works. The artist's wife and daughter form the base of a pyramidal composition, with the artist himself as its summit. The strictly frontal presentation of the figures, who are frozen into immobility, standing out against a background without depth or distinctive features, gives the work a solemn character and a timeless dimension that is disrupted by the presence of the open newspaper and the book, whose titles are clearly seen.
D.B.

Alexeï von Jawlensky
Torschov, 1864 - Wiesbaden, 1941

"Medusa", Head of a Woman
1923
Oil on cardboard
0.42 x 0.31
Acquired in 1956
Inv. 1956-24

Born in Russia, Jawlensky studied art in Munich, where, in 1909, together with Kandinsky, he founded the New Association of Munich Artists. Strongly influenced both by Fauvism and Expressionism, his work, from 1917 on, was marked by an almost exclusive preoccupation with the theme of the human face. In the early 1920s Jawlensky was working on the *Mystical Heads* and *Faces of the Saviour* series, as well as on the work shown here, also called *Light and Shadow*. Although Hélène Neznakomova, whom he married in 1922, most probably sat for this painting, the schematic nature of the representation does not suggest a portrait as much as an icon; it is in fact from the art of icon painting that the artist borrowed the codification of the face and its main features (here painted black), as well as the quest for permanency through repetition of a single theme in a series. Here the face occupies most of the painted surface, and the strikingly arbitrary use of pure colours lends it an extraordinary chromatic intensity. The overwhelming presence of the wide-open eyes (in opposition to the closed eyes of the faces where Jawlensky tends towards abstraction) strongly suggests the petrifying power of Medusa, one of the Gorgons, also alluded to in the sketched lines of the dishevelled hair. The spectator finds it difficult to withstand this truly hypnotic gaze.

C.B.

Marc Chagall
Vitebsk, 1887
Saint-Paul-de-Vence, 1985

Basket with Flowers
1927
Oil on canvas
1.165 x 0.735
Loaned by the Musée National d'Art
Moderne (*Dation* Chagall), 1990
Inv. 1990-84

In 1923, after working in the art school of Vitebsk, his native town, then for the Kamerny Jewish theatre in Moscow, Chagall left Russia with his family and settled in Paris in 1923. During his first exploratory years in France, he was commissioned by the dealer Ambroise Vollard to produce book illustrations. While working on La Fontaine's *Fables*, Chagall painted a number of luminous works on the theme of flowers or fruit. The painting shown here represents a large basket trimmed with mauve ribbons and loaded with fruit and branches, falling from the sky towards an open window. A small angel points to the person for whom the gift is intended: Bella, Chagall's wife, who is frequently celebrated in the artist's works. The high- angle view, as though seen from the sky, suggests that the painter is the potential donor of the basket, a metaphor of the lover's gift — but also the painter's — to the loved one. Chagall can thus play with differences in scale, a technique that, together with the levitation of objects and figures, he had been using since his "Russian years". The simplicity of the composition and the moving, dreamlike feeling give an intimate quality to this painting, which Chagall kept in his studio until his death.
C.B.

Pierre Bonnard
Fontenay-aux-Roses, 1867
Le Cannet, 1947

Flowers on a Mantelpiece at
Le Cannet
1927
Oil on canvas
1.05 x 0.75
Mr and Mrs Léon Bouchut Bequest,
1974
Inv. 1974-24

Immediately after moving, in February 1927, to Le Bosquet, a villa he had bought the previous year in Le Cannet, Bonnard painted a great number of interior views of his new house. The work shown here, presented at the Bernheim-Jeune gallery in the autumn of the same year, shows the fireplace of the small drawing room that Bonnard painted more than once, especially in the *White Interior* (1932) now in the Museum of Grenoble. The marble fireplace, shown frontally and off-centre, produces a network of orthogonal lines contrasting with and setting off a bunch of anemones in a vase; the same vase, in the same position, can be seen in a closer view of the room (1927), now in the Art Institute of Chicago. Along the edges, the artist has inserted other perspectives reduced to simple bands, which, by throwing the fireplace into the background, give a slight effect of depth. The cut-off figure of Marthe, the painter's wife, whose checked dress is also recognisable, is reminiscent of the bizarre centring techniques used in Japanese prints — which had a strong influence on Bonnard during the 90s — and of photography, which he himself practised. The whole of the painting is steeped in a warm Mediterranean light with vibrant harmonies of yellow and orange, in a radiant evocation of the pleasure of life.
C.B.

Pablo Picasso
Málaga, 1881 - Mougins, 1973

The Sideboard in
"Le Catalan"
1943
Oil on canvas
0.81 x 1.00
Gift by the artist, 1953
Inv. 1954-13

During the Second World War, Picasso, who was living in Paris, in Rue des Grands Augustins, frequented a restaurant called "Le Catalan", which was owned by a Spaniard who obtained his supplies on the black market. Picasso was struck by a brown sideboard with sculpted flutings which reigned over the dining room, and on 30 May 1943 he started work on two paintings based on this theme (the other of which is now in the Staatsgalerie in Stuttgart). There are two drawers, and above them is a bowl of cherries, some piled-up plates, and three glasses. The sobriety of the palette, which is dominated by dark brown, with turquoise and golden yellow highlights, is characteristic of Picasso's output during the Occupation. The cherry motif might be intended to commemorate his meeting, at Le Catalan, with Françoise Gilot, who was dining there with some friends, and who subsequently became his mistress: Picasso's first gesture had been to present her with a bowl of cherries. He donated the painting to the Museum of Fine Arts following the important, and very popular, retrospective that it devoted to him in 1953.
C.B.

Henri Matisse
Le Cateau-Cambrésis, 1869
Nice, 1954

Reclining Model, White Dress
1946
Oil on canvas
0.92 x 0.73
Loaned by the Musée National d'Art
Moderne (*Dation* Pierre Matisse),
1993
Inv. 1993-35

Contemporary with the large *Interiors*, painted between 1946 and 1948, in which Matisse gathered treasured objects and furniture, this *Reclining Model*, which, in some sense, can be linked back to the Odalisques of the 1920s, shows clearly the pleasure of the artist working with oils again after many years devoted to drawing; in 1947, Matisse wrote to André Rouveyre: "I feel all the curiosity I would have for a new country; I have never gone so far in the expression of colours." And indeed, in the paintings from those years, where he appears to be using the experience gained from his cut-up gouaches (*Jazz* was published in 1947), Matisse set up a new conception of space, as defined by the resources of colour alone.

The young woman, reclining on a cloak, forms a light-coloured diagonal which crosses the whole painting; she is shown from above within a space which appears to have developed from the small black rectangle formed by a door in the top right corner. This spatial enlargement highlights the wide, flat, red surface — a sort of velvet casing — on which the figure rests, devoid of all individual characteristics. Matisse painted another version of this figure at about the same time.

C.B.

André Masson
Balagny (Oise), 1896 - Paris, 1987

Niobe
1946-1947
Oil on canvas
1.78 x 1.40
Acquired in 1967
Inv. 1967-249

This painting, begun in 1946 and finished the following year, was intended to commemorate the sufferings of women and children during the war, as "a sort of monument to grief". The influence of Greek mythology, which is frequent in Masson's work, is fully justified by the commensurability of the legend with the artist's intentions: Niobe, wife of the king of Thebes, mourned the death of her seven sons and seven daughters, killed by Apollo and Artemis, so deeply that she turned to stone. The painter may also have drawn inspiration from Georges Duthuit's long poem about the occupation of Paris, *The Serpent in the Galley*, which he illustrated in 1945: "for the warrior's entertainment, there were Niobes on their knees by the side of the embankment, screaming with despair…". After such works as *The Burrow* (1946), which were directly linked to Masson's anguish about the war, 1947 marked, at one and the same time, a certain appeasement of his spirit and the beginning of a radical questioning of his painting; this was accompanied by, among other things, the disappearance of Greek mythology from his work.
D.B.

Jean Dubuffet
Le Havre, 1901 - Paris, 1985

Blond Landscape
1952
Oil on hardboard
1.14 x 1.46
Acquired from the artist, 1956
Inv. 1956-15

"In 1950", Dubuffet tells us, "with the *Landscapes of the Mental* and *Philosophical Stones*, which continued, with various ups and downs, to *the Materiologies* of 1960, I made more and more use of earth colours and of all the different ways to evoke physical phenomena in which the hand of man did not make any appearance". In the *Grounds and Terrains* series, to which this painting belongs, and which dates from May-July 1952, the thick "layers of paint suggest indefinable presences where the abolition of perspective makes all spatial representation ambiguous, to the point where it is difficult to decide if the space is that of an isometric view or that of a section such as those made by geologists" (Abadie). Painting no longer represents the world, but preserves matter in a state of trace, powder, mud; the image is swallowed up in it. But these soil effects, summarily manipulated, take on a symbolic and philosophical dimension — that of the earth from which we come and to which we return. The artist was delighted by the museum's purchase of this work, since it was the first time that a public institution had introduced a work by him into its collection.
C.B.

Nicolas de Staël
Saint Petersburg, 1914 - Antibes,
1955

The Cathedral
1954
Oil on canvas
1.90 x 1.30
Acquired with the help of the
F.R.A.M. in 1984
Inv. 1984-8

This work is often thought to have been one of de Staël's last creations, done shortly before his suicide; in fact, however, it was painted (if one may believe his friend Pierre Lecuire) not in Antibes but in Paris, during the summer of 1954. At this time the artist also painted a *Notre Dame* (private collection), inaugurating a theme of which *The Cathedral*, a powerful form emerging out of darkness, may have been the culmination. Standing out against a more fluid background, with mysterious harmonies of black and dark blue, the juxtaposition of light-coloured patches, each one imperfectly covering those that preceded it, links up once more with the vigorous technique of the 1952 *Roofs* (Musée National d'Art Moderne, Paris), with its similar concern for the ordering of space by rectangular planes.
C.B.

Sculptures
19th and 20th centuries
Chapel and Garden

Joseph Chinard
Lyon, 1756 - 1813

Perseus Rescuing Andromeda
Marble
H. 1.80; L. 0.77; Depth 0.80
Gift of Mrs Chinard, 1855
Inv. H 810

In 1786, Chinard became famous overnight when he won the competition organised by the Academy of Saint Luke in Rome, whith "The Deliverance of Andromeda" as its subject; it was very rare for a French artist to obtain such an honour. The terracotta model remained, and remains, the property of the academy; Chinard sent a plaster copy to Lyon, as a result of which the bursar, Jean-Antoine Terray, commissioned him to execute a life-size marble version. For unknown reasons, this marble was never finished; it remains, nonetheless, the best evidence of the sculptor's power of inspiration, which in this instance owes more to the French school, that of Julien and Pajou, than to Canova. For all that, the language is profoundly modern and original.

The museum also possesses a magnificent terracotta copy of this group, made by Chinard in 1791 during his second stay in Rome.
P.D.

Antoine Étex
Paris, 1808 - Chaville, 1888

Cain and his Race, Cursed by God
1832-1839
Marble
H. 2.05; L.1.71; Depth 1.53
Loaned by the State, 1839
Inv. H 807

The Salon of 1833 remains, for the history books, that of romantic sculpture. It was there that Barye exhibited his *Lion and Serpent*, and Rude his *Neapolitan Fisherman*. But it was Étex who enjoyed the greatest triumph, with the plaster model of this colossal group (now in the chapel of La Salpêtrière, Paris). The work was begun in 1831 in Rome, and its romantic inspiration was in all likelihood borrowed from Byron's 1821 play, *Cain*, combined with the stylistic influence of Michelangelo. It was popular with everyone, even Ingres, who did, nonetheless, denounce the dangers of a "sculpture of expression". In 1836, the state commissioned a marble version, which, immediately upon its completion, was handed over to the Museum of Fine Arts. The most direct descendant of this powerful work is no doubt Carpeaux's famous *Ugolin* (Musée d'Orsay).
P.D.

**James Pradier
(Jean-Jacques, called)**
Geneva, 1790 - Bougival, 1852

Odalisque
1841
Marble
H. 1.05; L. 0.94; Depth 0.61
Loaned by the State, 1841
Inv. H 793

This odalisque, which was exhibited in the 1841 Salon, is not only one of Pradier's finest nudes, but also a work of exceptional virtuosity, and also of great originality. Though the theme was in vogue at the time with painters and engravers (the influence of Ingres's earlier *Odalisque* is clear in this instance), it was much rarer in sculpture. The life-size representation of a nude seated directly on the ground, notwithstanding the orientalist pretext, was unacceptably daring for the classicists.
P.D.

Paul Chenavard
Lyon, 1807 - Paris, 1895

*The Social Palingenesis
(sketch)*
c. 1850
Oil on canvas
3.03 x 3.05
Loaned by the State, 1875
Inv. X 921-a

Immediately after the 1848 revolution, Chenavard was commissioned to do the interior decoration of the Pantheon, which was to be made into a temple of humanity. The artist resolved to represent the main stages of "the advancement of humankind through hardship and alternating periods of ruin and rebirth"; this is also expressed in the word "palingenesis". To carry through this cyclical concept, which was largely inspired by Hegel's philosophy of history, Chenavard intended to cover the walls with 60 grisaille paintings of large dimensions (a number of which are on show in the chapel of the museum) which would retrace significant historical moments, from the original chaos through to the French Revolution, while mosaics would present other scenes on the floors. The main mosaic, under the cupola, was intended to represent *The Social Palingenesis*, where Chenavard wanted to attempt an "impartial summary of every religious tradition". The circular composition, with more than 150 personages and symbols strongly influenced by ideas drawn from Freemasonry, is divided into three registers: *The Past*, dominated by the supreme divinity, *The Present*, with, in the centre of a portico, a syncretic image of the different religions, and *The Future*, which has been cut, but which was to represent the return of chaos, prelude to a renaissance of a superior humankind. Chenavard had been a student of Ingres, and this composition draws heavily on classical models (the influence of *The Dispute over the Holy Sacrament* and *The Athenian School* is obvious). After the 1851 coup by Napoleon III, the Pantheon was immediately restored as a Catholic church, and the project had to be abandoned; Chenavard, who had remained faithful to the ideals of 1848, never recovered from this setback.
C.B.

Chapel **19th century**

Auguste Rodin
Paris, 1840 - Meudon, 1917

*The Temptation of
St Anthony*
Before 1900
Marble
H. 0.62; L. 0.90; Depth 0.75
Acquired from the artist, 1903
Inv. B 661

On a plinth of almost disproportionate dimensions, a naked woman is reclining in a voluptuous pose on the back of the prostrate saint; the latter is dressed, unusually for Rodin, in a monk's frock. Passionately kissing the cross, the saint appears to be transferring his guilty desire to this religious object. The lasciviousness of the temptress does not, however, leave any doubt as to her sensuous nature. The back-to-back position of the figures is characteristic of a number of group sculptures by Rodin, who frequently combined works originally conceived separately in order to create new pieces. The woman is in fact taken from one of the figures of the *Gates of Hell*, which Rodin executed in 1889, and the dramatic atmosphere of the *Temptation* is closely linked to that of the *Gates*. Possibly inspired by Flaubert's *Temptation of St Anthony*, this marble, whose plaster version was shown at the large retrospective exhibition organised by Rodin at the Pavillon de l'Alma in 1900, is the first of the five works (two marbles and three bronzes) that the museum of Lyon purchased directly from the artist. C.B.

Auguste Rodin
Paris, 1840 - Meudon, 1917

Helmeted Minerva
1905
Marble
H. 0.54; L. 0.50; Depth 0.41
Acquired from the artist, 1906
Inv. B 763

This figure of classical beauty, a representation of wisdom, is also entitled *Minerva with a Helmet*. Rodin took his inspiration for this marble from the face of Mariana Russell, the wife of an Australian painter friend. René Cheruy, who was Rodin's secretary, remarked that the splendid Venetian helmet and the breastplate with the intertwined snakes were directly sculpted on the marble by Eugène Lagare, a student of the master and a highly skilled practitioner. There are a number of marble pieces by Rodin on the theme of Minerva in various collections, all apparently dating from 1900 to 1907.
C.B.

Émile Antoine Bourdelle
Montauban, 1861 - Le Vésinet, 1929

Carpeaux at Work
1909
Bronze
H. 2.53; H. 1.04; Depth 0.60
Acquired in 1910
Inv. H 810

It was in the Salon of the Société Nationale des Beaux-Arts in 1909 that Bourdelle exhibited this personal tribute to the author of the *Dance* group. The idea seems to have come to him as the result of a commission by Jacques Doucet for a bust of Carpeaux (now in the Jacques Doucet library, Paris). This was the most productive period in Bourdelle's career: it was also in 1909 that he planned the work which made him famous, *Heracles the Archer*, of which the museum also possesses a large bronze; the following year he began his décors for the Champs Élysées theatre. This *Carpeaux* would seem to have been a one-off casting, and its acquisition by the museum appears to have taken place in 1910.
P.D.

Joseph Bernard
Vienne, 1866
Boulogne-Billancourt, 1931

Tenderness
1912
Marble
H. 0.68; L. 0.48; Depth 0.42
Acquired from the artist, 1912
Inv. B 1020

The museum possesses an interesting set of works by Joseph Bernard, who was a student at the École des Beaux-Arts in Lyon from 1881 to 1886, before continuing his training in Paris. From 1906-1907 onwards, he was the prime mover in the return to sculpture done by directly cutting in stone or marble, without a preliminary clay or plaster model. This movement, which, for wood, was initiated by Gauguin, Lacombe and Maillol, aimed at a return, in the interests of sincerity, to the primary vocation of sculpture, namely that of the cutting away of material, as a reaction against the academic practice of modelling. Direct cutting was the method used for the execution of this particular group, which was presented at the 1912 Salon d'Automne, and which recalls, though in a new language, Rodin's celebrated *Kiss*. It derives from the couple in *Youth*, which was installed on the plinth of the monument to Michael Servetus in Vienne (France).

P.D.

Aristide Maillol
Banyuls-sur-mer, 1861
Perpignan, 1944

Venus
1918-1928
Bronze
H. 1.75; L. 0.63; Depth 0.39
Acquired in 1934
Inv. 1935-1

Goddess of beauty and love, this Venus is the outcome of a protracted project undertaken by Maillol without any precise objective, from a drawing: "I wanted to express in the sculpture what was to be found in the drawing — the same grandeur. But I had no intention of making a Venus…" The plaster model on which Maillol had been working since 1918 was shown in 1928 in the Salon d'Automne, where it met with universal approval. The fleshy fullness and massive proportions of the model secure this work a place among the artist's masterpieces. The graceful movement of the hands is explained by the fact that the young woman originally wore a necklace, which she was coquettishly raising. This casting of great beauty entered the museum the year the State started buying bronzes by Maillol for the national collections.
C.B.

Selected Bibliography

René Jullian,
La Sculpture du Moyen Âge et de la Renaissance,
catalogue du musée des Beaux-Arts de Lyon,
Lyon, 1945.

Madeleine Vincent,
La Peinture des XIXᵉ et XXᵉ siècles,
catalogue du musée des Beaux-Arts de Lyon,
Lyon, 1956.

Stéphanie Boucher,
Bronzes grecs, hellénistiques et étrusques des musées de Lyon,
Lyon, 1970.

Stéphanie Boucher,
Bronzes romains figurés du musée des Beaux-Arts de Lyon,
Lyon, 1973.

Quattrocento, Italie 1350-1523, peintures et sculptures du musée des Beaux-Arts de Lyon,
Lyon, 1987-1988.

Philippe Durey,
Le Musée des Beaux-Arts de Lyon,
Paris, 1988.

Marc Gabolde and Catherine Grataloup,
Les Réserves de Pharaon,
l'Égypte dans les collections du musée des Beaux-Arts de Lyon,
Lyon, 1988.

Dominique Brachlianoff,
De Géricault à Léger, dessins français des XIXᵉ et XXᵉ siècles dans les collections du musée des Beaux-Arts de Lyon,
Lyon, 1989.

Maria Van Berghe-Gerbaud and Hans Buys,
Tableaux flamands et hollandais du musée des Beaux-Arts de Lyon,
Paris-Lyon, 1991.

François Planet,
Le Médaillier, la monnaie, la cité, l'histoire,
Réunion des musées nationaux,
Paris-Lyon, 1992.

Valérie Lavergne-Durey,
Chefs-d'œuvre de la peinture italienne et espagnole, musée des Beaux-Arts de Lyon,
Réunion des musées nationaux,
Paris-Lyon, 1992.

Christian Briend,
Les Objets d'art, guide des collections,
Réunion des musées nationaux,
Paris-Lyon, 1993.

Hans Buys and Valérie Lavergne-Durey,
Catalogue sommaire illustré des peintures. t. I. Ecoles étrangères XIIIᵉ-XIXᵉ siècles,
Réunion des musées nationaux,
Paris-Lyon, 1993.

Index

Index   271

Photographic credits:
Alain Basset, Lyon
René-Gabriel Ojeda,
Réunion des musées nationaux, Paris
Laurent Sully-Jaulmes, Paris
All rights reserved

From the publications department
directed by Anne de Margerie

Editorial coordination: Gilles Fage,
Réunion des musées nationaux, Lyon
with the collaboration of Dominique Royer
and Laurence Barbier

Editing: Bernard Hœpffner
and Brian Holmes

Graphic design and layout:
atelier trois-quarts face, Lyon

This work was printed in
October 1995 on Satimat 135-g paper,
on the presses of the
Laffont printing house in Avignon.

Photo-engraving: Temps réel, Dijon

Binding: Alain, Félines.

Dépôt légal: novembre 1995
ISBN 2 7118 3205 8
GK 39 3205